I0131367

The StreetSmart Marketer

Book One:
11 Low-Cost Keys that Unlock the Secrets
To Rapid Growth in Your Business

Michael Hepworth

Manor House Publishing
www.manor-house.biz
905-648-2193

1

Library and Archives Canada
Cataloguing in Publication

CIP data for The Streetsmart Marketer:

Hepworth, Michael
     The streetsmart marketer / Michael Hepworth.

Contents: Bk. 1. 11 low-cost lessons to help business owners work less and make more.

ISBN 0-9781070-4-7 (bk. 1)

     1. Marketing--Management. 2. Small business--Marketing.
I. Title.

HF5415.H46 2006   658.8
C2006-905503-3

Cover photo: Courtesy of The StreetSmart Marketer
Cover design: Michael B. Davie

Copyright 2006: Michael Hepworth/Manor House Publishing
Published December 15, 2006
Manor House Publishing Inc. www.manor-house.biz
(905) 648-2193. First Edition. 144 pages. All rights reserved.

Imprint: Manor House

Manor House Publishing gratefully acknowledges the financial support of the Government of Canada through the Book Publishing Industry Development Program (BPIDP), Dept. of Canadian Heritage, for our publishing activities.

Foreword

A majority of small businesses fail, most within a few years of start-up, some after a generational change in management. Nearly two-thirds of such firms are owned or managed by women.

So, the odds are clearly stacked against Lindsay Roberts, the fictional heroine of Michael Hepworth's engaging *The StreetSmart Marketer: Book One: 11 Low-Cost Keys that Unlock the Secrets to Rapid Growth in Your Business*.

Hepworth, a leading expert on effective marketing techniques, for owner-operated businesses, skillfully combines an intriguing fictional story with terrific low-cost marketing advice that really works.

His information-packed book effortlessly educates and clearly explains marketing concepts and approaches in plain language.

This is a must-read for any business owner desiring fast growth and robust revenue. It takes marketing to a higher level.

When her father suddenly takes ill, Lindsay Roberts is thrust into running the quick print business her dad founded 25 years before. The business is in decline and she has no experience beyond five years of design and administrative work.

Desperate not to let the family down, she's working harder than ever and trying new things, but not much is working for her.

Frustrated and worried, Lindsay takes a break and by chance meets the StreetSmart Marketer. After a shaky start, the StreetSmart Marketer and Lindsay develop an easy relationship that leads to regular advice sessions covering the 11 Low-Cost Keys that Unlock the Secrets to Rapid Growth in Your Business.

By the end of the book Lindsay's father has recovered enough to come back to work, but barely recognizes the business he'd left six months earlier. Will this crusty Old School businessman take to the changes she's put in place? The adventure begins...

- **Michael B. Davie**, author, *Success Stories* and *Winning Ways*

Acknowledgements:

I dedicate this book to my loving wife and partner Madeline, to our children and loved ones and to all those who have helped us achieve success throughout our lives.

Special thanks to Michael B. Davie for editing, rewriting and other editorial services and for working closely with me in the crafting of this book. Our thanks to Canada: home, and land of opportunity. Many thanks as well to Manor House Publishing Inc. for helping make this writer's dream a reality.

- **Michael Hepworth**

About the Publisher

Founded in 1998, Manor House Publishing Inc. is today one of the most innovative business book publishers in North America.

For business leaders interested in creating a book, Manor House offers a virtual one-stop shopping experience, helping to develop books from concept to final edit version, and on to published and marketed hard copies. Manor House covers all production costs, revamps books for greater market appeal, places books in bookstores internationally, and makes books available to private purchasers at steep discounts. Manor House titles benefit from superb distribution networks providing worldwide market penetration, giving virtually all titles a global presence.

For more information, visit: www.manor-house.biz or email: mbdavie@manor-house.biz or phone: 905-648-2193.

About the Author:

Michael Hepworth is President of Results Exchange Group and founder/president of all *StreetSmart Marketer* enterprises.

Hepworth established the personal brand StreetSmart Marketer, along with proven marketing strategies that have helped thousands of clients achieve success.

Among other achievements, Hepworth developed a seven step process that starts with understanding who you're targeting and articulates what you do to resolve the potential clients' problems, discomfort or business pain; it involves working with people to overcome common mistakes – to help them grow at a rapid pace.

Hepworth and his wife Madeline are equal owners of his four-year-old rapidly growing Toronto-based business.

Michael Hepworth's previous experience includes managing and operating several prior successful companies – generating sales revenue of $39 million – that he sold at a profit, allowing him to live a financially independent lifestyle, doing whatever he wants to do, whenever he wants to do it.

Contact Michael Hepworth: streetsmart@streetsmartmarketer.com
Website: www.streetsmartmarketer.com or phone: 416-204-0353.

Contents

Manor House Publishing Inc.
www.manor-house.biz 905-648-2193

A Rough Introduction

L indsay Roberts re-read her emails. Again. She knew she was wasting time on trivial things to avoid facing her real business problems – if only she could clearly define them and find answers.

She was feeling stressed from 13-hour days with few breaks. Abruptly, she rose from her desk and reached for her jacket. Perhaps a coffee and a walk in the park would clear her head.

As she neared the front door, Lindsay caught a glimpse of her father's portrait in the hall. "Get well soon," she muttered under her breath. "I don't think I can handle your job much longer."

Several *Roberts Quick Printing Co.* staff members looked the other way as Lindsay walked by. They felt uncomfortable around the new boss. They missed Jack Roberts' confident charm, though it often masked the little print shop's difficulties in adapting to changing times. The staffers found the 32-year-old daughter a poor substitute for the man who founded the company 25 years ago and would still be at the helm if his fragile health would allow it.

Lindsay was now striding purposefully down the street to the coffee shop. She recalled how elated she'd been just a few months earlier when her dad asked her to take on running the firm while he followed doctor's orders to take it easy after a mild heart attack.

But that thrilling moment had ended abruptly when she saw the disappointment in his eyes. She realized her sudden promotion was owed solely to her status as his only child – there was no accompanying faith in her ability to run the company.

Lindsay cradled the hot cardboard cup in her hands as she made her way to the park across the street. In the shade of tall Maple there was an inviting park bench and discarded newspaper. She sat down and began reading the news as she sipped her coffee.

As she lowered the paper to turn the page, she was startled to find an older man in a business suit standing right in front of her. "Can I help you?" she glared, annoyed by the intrusion.

"Perhaps I can help *you*," the stranger replied. "I'm the StreetSmart Marketer."

"Wow, that's fascinating," Lindsay said sarcastically. The stranger smiled in response. He clearly wasn't getting the message that his presence was not required – or wanted. "You know," Lindsay added sharply, "you look a bit like that Michael Hepworth marketing guru in the business section." The man's smile widened.

"But he's much better-looking," she jabbed. Then she raised the newspaper to block her view of the stranger; an obvious signal the conversation was over.

Lindsay had resumed reading the newspaper. As she lowered it to turn the page, she was annoyed to find the smiling man still standing in front of her. He hadn't moved an inch.

"Look," Lindsay said angrily, "there better be a good reason why you're here."

"I came back to retrieve my newspaper – for the business section."

Lindsay's face flushed red with embarrassment. "Oh my Lord, I'm so stupid. I had no ideal. I'm so sorry. I feel terrible. I've been so rude to you, I, I, I don't know what to say… I'm, I'm…"

"A young businesswoman with marketing problems," the man said, completing her flustered ramble.

"It's that obvious?"

"That you're a young businesswoman?"

"No, that I have marketing problems."

The StreetSmart Marketer nodded. "Such problems are more common than you might think."

Lindsay smiled. "That's good to hear – I apologize that we got off to a rough start. Please forgive my earlier rudeness; I'm stressed out from running my Dad's business while he recovers from a heart attack. Things aren't turning out as I'd hoped – nothing's working. I thought some time away from the office might help me think more clearly... I'm Lindsay Roberts. You mentioned that you're the StreetSmart Marketer. I'd sure be interested in hearing any advice you can give me. I imagine you have some lessons I can learn, some keys to achieving success."

"Actually, if I can find time, I can share eleven keys that unlock the secrets to rapid growth in your business."

"Eleven?"

"Yes, I'm giving a speech in a few weeks and I've been writing down points I'll be covering. I have to leave now, but here's the course outline – hope you'll find it useful," he said, handing Lindsay a paper with 11 lessons in summary form.

Lindsay began reading the list. "This is amazing, when can we go over some of this?" she asked looking up from the list.

But the StreetSmart Marketer wasn't there...

StreetSmart Marketer's 11 Keys to Unlock Rapid Growth:

1. Ideal Prospects: All markets have ideal buyers. Focus resources on them: They're more profitable; easier to serve; readier to buy.

2. The Un-Written Marketing Rule: Advertising/marketing making the same claims as everyone else, makes customers focus on price. This only costs money, eroding margins and customer loyalty.

3. Fix the Product or Service First: You can't expect marketing to save a "me too" product or service. Businesses with generic or deficient products and services must first grasp what their market niche wants and then find ways to make the offer more compelling.

4. Sell the Bait First: To catch ideal buyers you have to use the right bait. People are resistant to being sold, but if you can first offer something free that your prospects want you have a much better chance of engaging them and selling them something.

5. Woo Prospects: Marketing, like dating, shouldn't be rushed. Marketers who ask for too big a commitment early on run the risk of scaring off otherwise interested parties.

6. Reverse The Risk: Risk causes hesitation and hesitation kills sales so Shoulder the risk. Up-front guarantees are a way of doing this.

7. Create Effective Advertising: Simply changing a headline has been shown to at least double or triple response rates.

8. Expanding Buying Behavior: Once a customer has bought from you, expand buying behavior as they're predisposed to buy again.

9. Repeat Mailings and Free Reports: If you only send a mailing out once you are only getting a fraction of the potential benefit.

10. Strategic Time Allocation: Being busy is the enemy of creativity and innovation. Entrepreneurs need to leave time for creativity and for working on the business, as well as in it.

11. Leverage and Mentoring: Leverage is the ability to create a large return with a small effort. Leverage can include mentoring.

KEY 1: Ideal Prospects

In all markets there are ideal buyers that are easier to sell than all other buyers. Focus your efforts and resources on ideal buyers: They are more profitable, easier to serve and more ready to buy.

It was early morning the following Thursday when Lindsay returned to the park cradling two cups of coffee and hopes of again meeting the mysterious stranger calling himself the StreetSmart Marketer.

She headed for the same park bench where they had met. Lindsay again found a waiting newspaper. But there was no sign of the StreetSmart Marketer. She was beginning to wonder if he'd ever really been there. Had the enormous stress she was under caused her to hallucinate?

Lindsay picked up the newspaper and immediately noticed a stick-on note that read: "I'm right behind you all the way, – SSM."

Thinking he might be by later, Lindsay began reading the paper when a thought suddenly occurred to her. She looked right behind herself to find the StreetSmart marketer standing there.

Lindsay laughed. "Are you sneaking up on me? Don't you make any sound when you walk, mystery man?"

The StreetSmart Marketer grinned in response. "Mystery man," he repeated. "I guess I should tell you I not only look like Michael Hepworth, I *am* Michael Hepworth and I like to keep a low profile – but I like to ensure my clients have the high profile. I'm more comfortable making sure they get the attention, not me."

"Your clients," Lindsay mused. "I've been meaning to ask you, what's your advice going to cost? I'm sure it's worth it, but I'd still like to know before we get started."

"At this point, I'll only charge one of those coffees," he said as Lindsay handed him one. "I've got time on my hands right now – and I enjoy chatting about marketing. In fact marketing and myself are my two favourite topics," he added with a grin. "So, there's no charge for the advice in this outdoor classroom – unless you want to move to a more formal setting like a boardroom."

"The park is fine," Lindsay smiled.

"Good. First of all, I need you to understand there is a process that you need to follow in order to be successful as a marketer. The 11 lessons I showed you last week follow that process. If you learn the process and apply your learning, you'll be successful. Now, tell me some of marketing difficulties you're encountering."

Lindsay described the circumstances of her sudden rise to acting company president, adding: "I really don't want to let my dad down, so I'm working harder than ever and trying new things, but not much is working for me."

Then, Lindsay described in more detail her frustrations in ineffectively dealing with a business in decline; her lack of managerial experience beyond her five years of design and limited administrative work; and, her biggest problem: her inability to successfully attract new customers and even keep some of her old ones despite peppering the entire business community with faxed and mailed flyers, and the company's sales reps visiting as many firms as possible. "And there's more," Lindsay added. "For..."

The StreetSmart Marketer held his hand up to signal a stop to Lindsay's diatribe. "Let's focus for now on the specific customer issue you just raised," he advised, "starting with a key consideration: who are you trying to sell to?"

"Everyone and anyone who buys printing," Lindsay replied.

"But how big is that number? In other words, how many people does that represent?"

"I don't know," Lindsay admitted, "but there are literally thousands of businesses – potential customers – within ten miles of our shop. I'm trying to reach as many of them as I can."

"What's your marketing budget?"

"Oh, I spend about $4,000 a month on marketing activities."

"So," the StreetSmart Marketer concluded, "that means you spend only a few cents per prospect each month! What's the likelihood of you getting noticed with all the competitors out there and all the advertising?"

"I can't afford to spend more on marketing," she protested.

"Agreed – but rather than spend more, why not spend what you're already spending, but spend it smarter? Instead of trying to reach the whole market and spreading your dollars so thinly they're completely ineffective, you should focus on a small segment of the market where you'll be noticed and where you can dominate. This brings to mind the story of the monkey trap used in Zimbabwe where money-eating tribesmen developed a simple but ingenious way to catch monkeys for food. They used gourds, which are like small pumpkins, but have a hard woody skin. If you put a small hole in the gourd, just big enough for a monkey to put his hand in and then remove the pulp inside, you have one of the most effective tools for catching monkeys. The tribesmen do this, and then place a few peanuts or kernels of corn inside and finally they fasten the gourd to a tree or a peg. Monkeys, being inquisitive, put their hands inside and grab hold of the food. However, once they have hold of it, they are unwilling to let go, and get caught. They refuse to let go even though they're terrified as the hunters approach. Logic doesn't enter into the equation."

"Interesting; how does it relate to marketing?" Lindsay asked.

"Well, many people try to serve everyone instead of specializing in a specific niche. This slows down growth. Prospects want to deal with specialists who are experts in their field. When you try to serve everyone you undermine this positioning. Others try to sell too many services and their message becomes diluted and hard to follow. We do this because we think having multiple offers and serving different markets covers the bases, when in fact the opposite is true. For most people this is counter-intuitive. They believe there is safety in serving multiple markets with multiple offerings. The problem is: most people won't specialize because like the monkey, they're scared of what they have to give up; they don't want to open their hand and let some of the market slip between their fingers, so they get stuck in the monkey trap. Yet if they let some of the market go, they'd be able to keep the rest, make it their own – and escape the trap. When you decide what you do and who you do it for, the funny thing is that the people you need to meet, do show up. To use another animal metaphor, you can't chase two rabbits; they both get away. Understand?"

As Lindsay nodded agreement, he continued: "In all markets there are ideal buyers that are easier to sell to than all of the other buyers out there. There are four traits of an ideal prospect: Do you know what they are?"

"They need what you sell – and they have money."

"Good start, but I believe there are four key attributes: They want your product; they have the ability to pay for your product; they have the authority to purchase your product; and, most importantly, they have bought products and services similar to yours before. If they have bought before it means they have an established need and have demonstrated a willingness to spend money to solve the problem. Contrast this with people who may have a need but have no interest in solving the problem."

"Can you give me an example of this?" Lindsay asked.

"Sure, when I was at school studying marketing, my lecturer told a story of two shoe salesmen who visited a poor African country to determine if there was a market for their products.
When they got there, each noticed almost no one wore shoes. One salesperson sent a telex back to his head office that stated: "This is a fantastic market – 90 per cent of the population does not wear shoes. I will be staying here an extra week to set up local agents." The other salesman also sent a telex to his office. This one read; "This is a terrible market; 90 per cent of the population doesn't wear shoes. I'll be returning on the next flight."

Lindsay looked perplexed. "So who was right?"

"In my view it was the second. Yes, there was a need, but the people were not predisposed to buying. To win in that market, you would have to educate people about the reasons for wearing shoes and change the culture. Not a very easy task. Realize also that customers that have previously purchased from you are more likely to do so again, while firms that don't know you and may not have significant printing needs are less likely to buy. Focus mainly on ideal buyers as they are more profitable, easier to serve and more ready to buy from you."

"Should I just ignore the less-then-ideal buyers?" she asked.

"We're not at that stage yet. We've first got to figure out who you want to focus on."

"So, I should sort the customers out into groups, mainly concentrating on the ideal buyers, while still reaching out to the next group with good potential and spending a lot less time on those who are much less likely to buy?"

"I'm not saying don't do business with people outside this ideal prospect group. In fact in your current situation that might be dangerous. I'm saying concentrate all of your resources on finding and acquiring customers from your ideal prospect group."

Lindsay smiled. She now knew the ideal prospect population for her printing business was much smaller than she'd realized.

"Essentially," the StreetSmart Marketer continued, "you need to target the ideal buyers to get more customers. At the risk of being repetitive, every market has a smaller number of ideal buyers as opposed to all buyers. Ideal buyers are: easier to sell; easier to serve; more profitable; generate more referrals – and they're likely to become the best clients. Focusing on the relatively few prospects who will probably be high revenue generators allows you to concentrate your resources on this critical group. In practice this means investing your marketing budget in pursuing the potential customers who will generate the most revenue. Your investment per prospect is your total marketing budget divided by the number of ideal buyers."

"So…" Lindsay said hesitantly, "suppose I do target the ideal buyers – how do I actually go about turning them into customers?"

"To convert best buyers into customers, you must target them consistently and ferociously. This is a five stage process in which you shift your prospect's attitude to your favour. The five stages the prospect can experience are as follows: One: 'I've never heard of this person'. Two: 'Who is this person?' Three: 'I think I've heard of this person'. Four: 'Yes! I've heard of this person'. And, five: 'I want to meet this person'. You basically help them make the transition from having never heard of you to wanting to get to know you and do business with you."

"Impressive – but isn't it a lot of work?" Lindsay suggested.

"It can be," the StreetSmart Marketer concurred.

"But remember, the best clients are the easiest and most profitable to service. They buy more, spend more, and refer more. Therefore, the amount of time and effort you spend cultivating them is apt to generate far greater rewards than you'd achieve with even greater efforts with other clients."

"I may need to change the way we do things..."

"Perhaps so – but that's not as daunting as it sounds," the StreetSmart Marketer advised. "If you focus on your ideal customers' needs, you automatically tailor your business to meet their needs. Also, ideal customers buy faster, and in shortening the selling cycle you generate sales revenue sooner and at less cost. And by increasing the frequency at which your best clients buy from you, you can grow your business faster."

"So things start to fall into place," Lindsay pondered.

"Exactly," the StreetSmart Marketer smiled. "Once you have satisfied the best buyers, you have qualified yourself in two important ways. First, you can sell them more. And second, by asking them for referrals you can acquire more clients like them — the best clients."

"And I should really focus my marketing dollars on this ideal group," Lindsay considered, "as the best buyers offer a lot more bang for my buck…"

"They sure do," the StreetSmart Marketer agreed, "and you can accomplish much more by dedicating your budget on the people who give you the best results. For example, let's say you have 1,000 prospects and a monthly marketing budget of $10,000. If you target all prospects, you can spend $10 per prospect. However, if you target the critical 10 per cent, the ideal buyers, you can spend your $10,000 on only 100 prospects. How much more marketing can you do for $100 per prospect?"

"A lot," Lindsay grinned. "Oh, I'm sorry, that was a rhetorical question, wasn't it?"

"It started out as a rhetorical question – but you've made a personal question that you've answered with enthusiasm – and I certainly can't fault you for that. In fact, it's terrific that you're really taking this to heart and finding ways you can apply these concepts to your business."

"I can see this approach making a huge difference with prospects," Lindsay enthused. "And likely customers too?"

"Yes, absolutely. Once prospects become customers, the same considerations apply. How much better service can you provide if you focus on totally satisfying 200 ideal customers rather than simply serving 1,000? Clearly it is easier and less expensive to understand and meet the needs of 200 ideal customers than to try the same thing with 1,000."

"How do I figure out who my ideal prospects are?" she asked.

"Well, apart from the four characteristics I mentioned a few moments ago, most of the answers lay inside your business: You need to look at your client base and see who your most profitable customers are, who are the easiest to sell, who does the most repeat business with you, who are the most fun to serve? Also look at where you have a competitive edge, and so on. You need to do this kind of analysis before you can go much further. You need to see if you can find a well targeted niche that you want to target. You can design every aspect around satisfying that need."

Lindsay looked puzzled. "What do you mean?"

"I know you don't sell hamburgers, but let me give you an example: Who do you think McDonalds target customers are?"

"Children, people in a rush…"

I don't know this for certain, but I believe it's families with small children. Everything about their business is geared to serving this group. That's why they have play areas, provide toys with the meals, market the kind of food they serve, and so on. You have to know who you are serving and understand specifically how your product solves their pain and how to communicate that to them. You can't do this if you serve everyone. There's an axiom in marketing that's important to remember; "If you sell everyone you sell no one and if you sell everything you sell nothing."

"That's right," Lindsay confirmed, "we don't do any marketing beyond sending out basic flyers. We depend instead on networking and referrals to get our customers."

The StreetSmart Marketer smiled. "Lindsay, networking and referrals are part of marketing. Once you know who your ideal prospect is, it gives networking more purpose. You go where you are most likely to meet prospects or people who already know who you need to know. In fact, potentially the most important question you can ask yourself is: "Who already knows the people I need to know?" The answers to that question can be a shortcut to many lead-generating activities."

"Just about everything seems to be marketing…"

"Lindsay, a lot of people don't understand that anything you do to attract and keep business is marketing. This key understanding is important because when you grasp that, you begin to realize that we're all marketing – then you can assess whether your marketing is effective or ineffective. It's surprising how many times I'll hear someone proudly state they don't do any marketing. In fact, I hear this fairly often from professional services businesses. In many cases I believe this to be because people are scared to do what they don't know or understand, and for many professionals, marketing is scary unknown territory. It need not be if you learn a few basic principles, but many people find it easier to believe they don't market or to believe they have found the "secret sauce" that means they don't need to market."

Lindsay nodded agreement while the StreetSmart Marketer continued. "Lindsay, you mentioned you rely predominantly on networking and referrals. To me, marketing is everything a business does to acquire and keep customers. So in my book networking and referrals definitely fall into marketing and are not the cost-free tactics they might appear to be. In fact, I believe that these two tactics are often the default for people who have no marketing strategy or process. While these tactics can create quite a successful business, they eventually limit your growth because ultimately the amount of networking you can do is limited."

"How so?"

"Well, for one thing, when you are networking you can't deliver, and when you are delivering, you don't have time to network. If these are your only marketing tools, it will be extremely difficult to grow your business beyond a few customers. The truth is that networking and referrals have lots of hidden costs that are actually marketing costs. For example: lunches, dinners, coffee, membership fees, meeting attendance, your time, travel etc. Don't think your time is free. It isn't; it's probably your scarcest and most valuable asset as a business owner. If you don't revere your time, your customers never will. And remember, there is also an opportunity cost to doing these things."

Lindsay's eyes widened. "I hadn't considered the real costs in money and time that I have to pay for networking and referrals."

The StreetSmart Marketer gave a reassuring smile. "You're not alone in that department – many people don't take the real costs into consideration. But, by doing all these activities, the costs add up. You'll be surprised to discover how much a new customer really costs you, even with these seemingly free activities. Calculate how much you spend on the items I've mentioned each year. Once you know all of your "marketing" expenses for the year, divide that number by the number of new customers you get each year. You might be surprised at how high the number is."

"This is all quite an eye-opener," Lindsay acknowledged. "I've just done a very rough calculation in my head, and those lunches and other costs really add up."

"That's what you spend buying customers each year," the StreetSmart Marketer explained, "and the danger in not initially understanding this is twofold. First, there may actually be cheaper more efficient ways of marketing your business, but without any understanding of the costs, how can you tell? Second, if you think of your activities as free, you don't look at them as an investment in creating and keeping customers and this alters your behaviour on marketing and client service – I believe you take it less seriously than you should."

"But it's really a costly investment," Lindsay ventured.

"Exactly," the StreetSmart Marketer confirmed. "The first step is to recognize that you've invested large sums of money over the years of building your business. I believe marketing is simply a way of buying customers. For some people this may sound distasteful, but you should try to get used to it. Simply put, whether you acknowledge it or not, your business buys customers. If you get better at marketing than your competitors, it becomes cheaper for you to acquire each customer than it does for your competitors and the more customers you get. And, you can become a good deal more selective in the type of customers you acquire."

"The idea of buying customers will take a bit of getting used to, but I can see that's just what I'm doing," Lindsay considered.

"Reaching that realization, as you've just done, is an important step," the StreetSmart Marketer advised. "Once you see marketing and client acquisition as an investment, it leads you to ask yourself: How do I protect that investment? And, how do I optimize that investment?"

"I don't know how to thank you," Lindsay said. "You've given me a wealth of information, a lot of very good advice. I just hope I can remember it all…"

"Not to worry," the StreetSmart Marketer said, handing her a slip of paper. "I've prepared some notes on figuring out who the ideal prospects are."

"I just want to say that these points are very interesting – and effective," Lindsay said, looking up from the notes.

But once again, the StreetSmart Marketer had disappeared.

KEY 1: Ideal Prospects: Summary

1. In all markets there are ideal buyers that are easier to sell than all other buyers. Focus your resources mainly on ideal buyers, as they're more profitable, easier to serve and more ready to buy.

2. Ensure prospects buy from you and not your competition, by tailoring your approach to fit their needs. Instead of pestering them with calls asking them if they're ready to buy, keep in touch with them by providing useful information they can use. You then emerge as their first choice when they are ready to do business.

3. Understand that marketing is everything a business does to acquire and keep customers; then work to make your marketing efforts more effective.

4. Networking and referrals are part of marketing. These two tactics are often the default for people who have no marketing strategy or process. While these tactics can create quite a successful business, they eventually limit your growth because ultimately the amount of networking you can do is limited. When you're networking you can't deliver, and when you're delivering, you don't have time to network. If these are your only marketing tools, it will be extremely difficult to grow business beyond a few people.

5. Networking and referrals have lots of hidden costs that are actually marketing costs. For example, lunches, dinners, coffee, membership fees, meeting attendance, your time, travel etc. Don't be fooled into thinking your time is free. It isn't. And remember there is also an opportunity cost to doing these things.

6. By doing all these activities, costs mount up and you will be surprised to discover how much a new customer really costs you, even with these seemingly free activities.

7. Whether you acknowledge it or not, your business buys customers. The first step is to recognise that you have invested considerable sums of money over the years of building your business and understand that marketing is simply a way of buying customers. For some people this may sound distasteful, but you should try to get used to it.

8. Marketing and client acquisition is an investment. In order to protect that investment, you have to do everything to ensure that once acquired, a customer comes back regularly to buy more. This is true in businesses where clients only buy once or occasionally. Even in businesses where marketing is restricted to networking and referrals, client acquisition is still the most expensive thing you do. The best way to protect this investment is to fall in love with your customer rather than with your product or service. Falling in love with your customer will ensure you provide service that is without peer.

2

"The greatest obstacle to discovery is not ignorance – it is the illusion of knowledge."
- **Daniel J. Boorstin**

"In writing, if summarizing is death, details and specifics provide life."
- **Michael Masterson**

KEY 2: The Unwritten Marketing Rule:

Differentiate yourself from competitors. Advertising and marketing that's the same as everyone else's does as much for your competitors as it does for you. Marketing that makes the same claims as everyone else, forces customers to focus on one thing they do understand; price. This results in eroding margins and a lack of customer loyalty.

The following week, Lindsay was again walking briskly to the park – but with a very confident spring in her step – to meet up with the StreetSmart Marketer for what was now a regularly scheduled meeting.

She found him walking towards their favourite park bench, newspaper tucked under his arm.

"Hello Mr. Hepworth, my StreetSmart Marketer knight in shining armour," she greeted him. "You've really rescued me from a lot of bad practices – I've been following your advice and it really works. Things are getting turned around for the better, bit by bit. It's absolutely amazing, when you know where to start, what you can accomplish."

"Oh, I can't take all the credit for rescuing you," came the modest reply. "You've really done the work and rescued yourself. All the good advice in the world doesn't do much good unless you're prepared to put in the hard work to carry it out."

As they walked side-by-side to the bench, Lindsay handed him a coffee and nervously cleared her throat. "I guess you haven't met many people like me – I'm a bit of an odd duck," Lindsay suggested uneasily, "because while I was good at my old job – or at least I think I was – I really wasn't ready to take on the whole business. I really didn't think the business would be so much more difficult and…"

"Actually," the StreetSmart Marketer gently interrupted, "I meet many people during the course of my work who go into business for themselves, simply because they are good at what they do. Take Susan, for example, a physiotherapist who loves what she does. She worked in a multi-disciplinary clinic for some years before branching out on her own. Because she was good and she was in demand at the clinic, she believed the same would be true if she went out on her own."

"And was it the same?"

"No, once Susan went out on her own, she found it to be quite different. She brought in a modest amount of business, but could never quite reach the level she wanted. She felt she couldn't really afford qualified staff, so she spent her days dealing with patients and her evenings doing administration. To put it bluntly, she was working like a dog, but was flat broke."

Lindsay sighed. "Sounds familiar... what happened next?"

"Well, she began to realize that being good at physiotherapy was a table stake. If she didn't learn to market she would never break out of the 'busy and broke' mould so many business owners find themselves in. She felt uncomfortable with marketing because she comes from a world where marketing is frowned upon. It's almost a dirty word. Most of her colleagues believe that if you are good you don't have to hype what you do."

"Wow," Lindsay said in the low voice, "that must be really hard when your peers take the view that marketing is unseemly and unnecessary – were you able to help her?

The StreetSmart Marketer nodded. "I spent time with her showing that this idealistic view is somewhat naive. There are simply so many people her patients could go to for the same service that she wasn't even on the radar. She had to understand that her job was to get her message to her patients, because they certainly weren't going to go looking for her."

"And did she... reach this understanding?

"Yes, here's what she did: Her first step was to figure out why she is different. She discovered that most of her patients were young, athletic executives. They came to her because she understood sports injuries. And she understood the competitive nature of these people. Her business was different because she specialized in getting these go-go people back in action quickly."

The StreetSmart Marketer took a sip of coffee and continued. "Her next step was to build her reputation as a specialist in this field. She started speaking to groups of executives, she wrote articles, she held special events and she built a content rich website to serve them."

"Impressive," Lindsay said appreciatively.

"Absolutely, but then came the hard part for her; generating leads. She started a referral program with her existing patients; she ran a successful direct mail campaign and developed alliances with two gyms that have a high number of young executive members. The combination of these simple strategies created a steady stream of five to eight new leads per week."

"Very impressive."

"There's more: Susan next hired a receptionist/admin assistant to take on some of the administrative load and had her make calls to follow up all the leads that were coming in. Susan resisted this at first, as she didn't think she could afford it. But when her new assistant began to bring in about 30-50 per cent of the people she followed up with, Susan realized this wasn't a cost, but was instead an investment in growing her business. Today, she is thinking of bringing in another physiotherapist into the business and she's also looking at hiring a masseur."

The StreetSmart Marketer took another sip of coffee. "The point is: if you are in business for yourself, you must develop a lead machine. Simply relying on passive referrals from happy clients will bring in a certain amount of business but you'll never make much that way. You will most likely join the ranks of the busy and broke. Don't let this happen to you."

"I won't," Lindsay promised. "I guess it's never enough to simply offer great products or services – you always have to market too."

"Exactly," the StreetSmart Marketer confirmed, with a mischievous grin. "After all, I hate to be the bearer of bad news, but there are other companies out there that offer the same products or services that you do. Of course, you already know that, but what are you doing about it? It's a simple fact of life that everybody is in competition with everybody else. This means unless you are better than your competition – or at least equal to them – you are in a dangerous position and you should probably get out of the business. This may sound harsh, but it is the reality."

"I'm finding that it certainly is a very competitive world out there," Lindsay agreed. "I don't know if there are any shortcuts to success, but…"

"I often say," the StreetSmart marketer gently interjected, "that the secret to being successful in business is that there is no secret. You simply have to do a lot of things well. Everything counts. Don't be lulled into thinking that some of the things you do don't count or are unimportant. They may be to you, but how can you be sure your customers and prospects feel that way? Every moment of truth either adds to the experience or takes away. Everything either helps or hinders. Nothing is neutral."

"Every little thing counts?"

"Yes – and when you understand this you are beginning to develop the winning edge. In the Olympics, athletes win by millimetres and milliseconds. The same is true in business. Minute differences make all the difference when it comes to winning business. You'll know when you provide the best value because people vote with their wallets."

"So how do you improve to the point where your product or service is a winner?"

"The simplest way is by asking yourself a series of questions designed to reveal real value. Start by asking: What's selling well right now in my market? The answers to this question can be uncovered via search engines, trade journals, magazines, television, top 10 lists, and simply by listening and observing. Then ask: What's missing from these products/services? And when you've answered that one, ask yourself: How can I improve my existing product or service to make it a winner? Question three then becomes a jumping off point for a whole series of questions you can ask yourself to improve your product or service. One question that's sure to arise is: What can we add to the product?"

"Can you give me an example?" Lindsay asked.

"Sure: my last notebook computer had an external wireless card. This was a nuisance as it had to be removed for travel. My latest laptop, bought only a few weeks ago, now has wireless capability built in – a major additional improvement – and on top of that, it has a whole lot of new features that I hadn't expected."

"Might you also ask what can we take away from the product?" Lindsay wondered.

"Yes, staying with my laptop, I now have a machine that is several pounds lighter than my previous one – they took away a lot of weight. How they achieved that I don't know, but it certainly makes a difference."

"Would another question be: Can we change the way people use the product?"

"Absolutely – and that's a good question to ask. Here's an example of changing the way a product is used: People are now using exercise balls for office chairs to improve their posture. Another good question to ask is: Can we change the market? The answer again is yes. An example: Once primarily a business tool, cell phones are now being offered as safety tools for young children. More good questions: Can we change the price? And, is there a way to make buying easier for our clients? Well, instalment plans work, so do unbundled products."

Lindsay smiled. "That's a lot of questions…"

"There's more: Can we bring back something from the past? The retro styling of the Mini Cooper and VW Beetle are perfect examples of this kind of thinking. Can we alter the size? Well, remember the days when a cell phone was the size of a brick? Now they are tiny little pocket devices. Can we do creative things with colour? My wife went into buy a cell phone the other day and came back with a bright pink one. And of course there are many other examples, many other ways of answering these questions."

"How should I deal with these questions?" Lindsay asked.

"Over the next few days, review your product or service against these questions, these criteria. Make them into a check list and each time you have a spare moment, spend some time thinking about how to create a winning product or service in your market place by asking and then answering each of the questions posed."

"You can never do too much marketing," Lindsay surmised.

"Actually, you can do too much *ineffective* marketing – and marketing clutter is making every business owner's life much tougher. According to marketing authority Chet Holmes, decision makers are now exposed to 30,000 commercial messages daily, as compared to only 3,000 such messages ten years ago. Similarly, the cost of selling has almost tripled over the past decade. It now takes 8.4 attempts on average for a sales representative to get in front of a prospect, whereas 10 years ago, it took only four tries. In today's market, salespeople must work three times as hard to achieve half the results they used to. Despite these averages, most salespeople give up after only two attempts at contacting a prospect. Yet the star performers continue to be successful. Thus, most prospecting efforts are wasted, lost in all the clutter."

"What can a business owner do about this?" Lindsay asked.

"My first suggestion is to engage your prospects, by providing them with important market information that helps them become better buyers. This can be achieved – by mailing or e-mailing to your target list – with the offer of a free report with a title such as; 'The 3 Greatest Dangers Facing (customer name here) and what You Can Do To Survive Them'."

"Sounds like a very effective way to do things."

"It is," he agreed, "but do not send the report out unsolicited. Once those people who are interested contact you to request the information, you can begin the necessary sales dialog."

"In addition, you need to make sure your salespeople know the average number of contacts required to be successful and follow up accordingly. You can then set up a policy for the number of contacts required and a process of sequential marketing activities to help your salespeople deal with each way a contact might turn out. Simply put, you have to provide everyone on your team with the tools to enable them to perform like a superstar."

"That's a fairly scientific approach," Lindsay observed.

"Yes, but you have to remember that business prospects are people too and that they sometimes make purchases for emotional reasons. When marketing to them, remember these three emotional appeals, and include them in your sales pitches and in your copy: First: the fear of failure: When using this appeal you can be direct and address the possibility that they may fail if they don't take advantage of your services. Second: A desire for recognition: Here you have an opportunity to focus on their dreams and desires for career success and how your service can help them achieve it. Third: A desire for a stress-free existence. This is a simple and straight forward emotion to address when dealing with business people. Show how implementing what you recommend can help provide them with a stress-free existence. Remember to focus as much on the human side of your prospect as you do on the business side – and you will find it will pay off in spades."

"I think you've just pinpointed something I'm a little guilty of at times," Lindsay admitted. "I often tend to focus heavily on the business side of things and not so much the human side; I tend to promote our services and strengths rather than zeroing on ways to make life easier for the customer or prospect; rather than focusing on their wants and needs."

"It's a very good thing to recognize such problems," the StreetSmart Marketer reassured her, "and what you've just described is actually part of a much larger problem – the tendency for business owners to engage in *Me Marketing* instead of *You Marketing* – and you're certainly not alone in that regard."

"What do you mean by that?" Lindsay asked.

"Let me explain: During the course of a week, I usually meet several people who hope to sell me something – what astonishes me is how few of these people ask questions to find out what I am interested in or worried about. Most start with a pitch aimed at impressing me with their success. I hear about all the amazing customers they have… Then they tell me all about the wonderful technology they have, or how marvelous their products or services are… by this time I have generally lost interest. It is such a shame that these otherwise competent people shoot themselves in the foot and most lose the opportunity to sell me something because they're so focused on themselves and have little understanding or feeling for what I might be interested in. I call this *Me Marketing*. It is a lot more common than most of us realize and destroys more sales than almost any other mistake."

"*Me Marketing*," Lindsay repeated. "Interesting concept."

The StreetSmart Marketer continued: "I often compare *Me Marketing* failures to the boastful approach taken by an arrogant suitor: It is like bragging about your possessions or achievements in the hopes that you will impress your date. In most cases all it achieves is boredom, or even worse, it turns your date off completely. This approach has the same effect with prospects."

"Yes – I can see that," Lindsay agreed. "I really get turned off by a salesman's bragging – and I hate to admit it, but I sometimes do too much bragging myself."

"Well, recognizing the problem of *Me Marketing* is the first step to solving it. In sharp contrast, StreetSmart Marketers engage in *You Marketing*. They make sure that all their marketing materials focus first on customer issues before their capabilities and competencies. They never pitch without first building rapport. Above all they know that customers don't buy from them because they have the best products and services, but because they understand them as people. Their marketing is designed to demonstrate that understanding."

"Thank you," Lindsay murmured, "I can see how *You Marketing* is much more effective."

"The key thing to keep in mind is that success is built on positive relationships: The truth is, people buy from people they like, and we generally like people who are interested in us and our needs. In most cases, as potential buyers, we're completely selfish and will only engage if we find something or someone to be interesting. Successful salespeople quickly learn that you can't be interesting unless you are interested."

"And a good way to show interest is to ask questions to find out more about the customer or prospect?" Lindsay asked.

"You've got it," the StreetSmart Marketer confirmed with a smile. "StreetSmart Marketers know the best way to demonstrate interest is to ask insightful questions as they ultimately provide insightful answers in their marketing communications, showing customers how they are the logical choice to solve some burning problem. Once they understand these challenges they use their knowledge and skills to raise perception about potential solutions. Only then do they introduce the product or service and what it can do for the client."

With that, the StreetSmart Marketer handed Lindsay a summary sheet, covering key points of their discussion, and advised: "I have to leave now to meet up with some friends – thanks for the coffee – we'll meet again in a week's time."

"Well, thank you so much," Lindsay smiled widely, as she watched him walk away. "I'll be putting all of your points into practice right away."

KEY 2: The Unwritten Marketing Rule

1. Realize that simply offering a valuable service or product is not enough to succeed. You need to market your product or service to bring customers to you.

2. Figure out what makes your business different or unique. Then, differentiate yourself from competitors. Advertising and marketing that's the same as everyone else's does as much for your competitors as it does for you. Marketing making the same claims as everyone else, forces customers to focus on one thing they do understand; price. This leads to an eroding of margins and a lack of customer loyalty.

3. To generate leads, use a combination of strategies, such as starting a referral program, utilizing direct mail campaigns and developing alliances with businesses whose services complement your own.

4. If you cannot find the time to personally deal with incoming business sales and opportunities, hire an administrative assistant to take on some of the load. It's a false economy to think you're saving money by not hiring – when in fact an assistant may well secure sales revenue far in excess of their salary.

5. Strive to increase sales by improving your product or service. You can effectively do this by first asking yourself a series of questions concerning ways the product might be improved, from lowering the price to adding features and benefits that add value and desirability.

6. Avoid having your marketing efforts lost in the clutter of unwanted advertising messages and sales pitches. Instead, get to know your prospects and customers; provide them with gifts of value – such as information they can use, educate them on the value of your service – *then* sell them.

7. Tailor the free information reports you send customers to meet their needs and concerns. But don't send such reports unsolicited. Get the client to request the report. This gives you an excuse to follow up in a friendly manner with more information that helps educate the customer into becoming a better buyer while matching them with the right products and services, virtually guaranteeing repeat business.

8. Practice *You Marketing* focusing on the customer's needs and goals rather than *Me Marketing* focusing on how highly you think of your products and services. The customers and prospects don't care if you think you're the best; what they do care about is whether what you're offering meets their specific needs and will help them achieve success. Don't be guilty of bragging to the bored.

9. Success is built on positive relationships: People buy from people they like, and we generally like people who are interested in us and our needs. In most cases, as potential buyers, we're completely selfish and will only engage if we find something or someone to be interesting. Successful salespeople quickly learn that you can't be interesting unless you are interested.

10. The best way to demonstrate interest is to ask insightful questions as they ultimately provide insightful answers in marketing communications that show customers why you are the logical choice to solve burning problems. Once StreetSmart Marketers understand these challenges they use their knowledge and skills to raise perception about potential solutions. Only then do they introduce the product or service and what it can do for the client.

3

"Business has only two functions – marketing and innovation."
-Milan Kundera

"Excellence is not an exception, it is a prevailing attitude."
 - Colin L. Powell

KEY 3: Fix the Product or Service First:

You can't expect marketing to save a "me too" product or service. You have to be the buyers' first choice. Businesses with generic or deficient products or services must find ways to understand what their market niche wants; then find ways to make the offer more compelling to prospects.

When Lindsay next met the StreetSmart Marketer, he was pacing around in a circle in front of their park bench meeting place in the shadow of a stretching maple tree.

"Hello Mr. Hepworth – you seem a bit preoccupied."

"I suppose I am, Lindsay. I keep thinking about why falling in love with your product can be dangerous to your wealth!"

"What do you mean by that?" Lindsay asked, as she handed him a coffee and a napkin.

"Well, twice in the past week, budding entrepreneurs have told me they're starting a business and each of them has eagerly told me something like: 'I have a great idea; no one else is even thinking of it; there are no competitors. I just know I can make a lot of money if I can get it to market! Will you help me market it?' Neither of them has any business ownership experience, but both have a lot of enthusiasm…"

"No competitors," Lindsay interjected. "Sounds wonderful."

"Perhaps, but perhaps not," the StreetSmart Marketer mused between sips of coffee. "You see, each believes they can be successful, but in both cases I am uncertain. Not because I think what they want to sell won't sell. I just don't know – and I wouldn't sink my money or time into either idea at this stage."

"What are they trying to market?" Lindsay asked.

"Unfortunately I can't reveal what they want to sell, as that would be unfair. I can tell you that one is involved with a branch of management consulting and the other is a software product. But what is more useful, is to share with you why I think what they are doing is risky and how they might go about finding a better way."

"So how is it risky?"

"While it is possible to make money with a new product that no one has thought of before, I believe their approach is risky because there is no ready, established demand that you can tap into – simply because the product is new and hasn't found a market."

Lindsay nodded appreciatively. "I hadn't thought of that – but it makes perfect sense. They want to introduce products that are untried in the marketplace, without knowing how many people might buy them. Had they done any market research?"

"That's certainly something I wanted to find out and I had a number of questions. My first question was: 'What makes you so sure anyone will buy what you are selling?' One said he just knew it in his gut, the other said she had spoken to friends about it and they just loved the idea. Both of these are dangerous reasons to believe your business idea will make you rich."

"They really had nothing solid to suggest their unique ideas would fly? Lindsay questioned.

"Exactly. Many people look for the unique idea – but I would rather sell a product for which I know there is significant demand, even if there are a lot of competitors. There is always room for another competitor especially if you are better than the others."

"So having a unique idea isn't always a big advantage," Lindsay concluded.

"Correct. What is more important than a unique idea is to make your entire business unique in ways that are important to your prospects. So, for example, as a printer, what reasons should people do business with you and not your competition? The ways your prospects find you are unique could be in your price, or in your process, or in your materials, or in any of a dozen elements of your business."

"And I suppose," Lindsay pondered, "even if your idea is a good one, you're not going get far unless other people like it too and are willing to purchase or invest in making it happen?"

"That's right, Lindsay. The first thing to remember about customers; is that they vote with their cash. Unless you can find someone who will pay you cash for your idea, then it may be nothing more than simply an idea. Gut feeling is a poor substitute for positive proof that someone is willing to give you cash. Friends, although well intentioned, can also be misleading. They want to please and they are seldom your target market, so their advice is at best subjective."

The StreetSmart Marketer took another sip of coffee and continued. "Not only that, if it is a new idea and no one has what you are selling then how do you know there is a market? This is a common mistake that people make: They fall in love with an idea and expect the market to do the same. I would much rather sell a product for which I know there is a ready demand. If you were selling men's suits, would you rather sell them to people who occasionally wear a suit for work because suits are making a comeback or would you be better off looking for people who wear a different suit every day of the week? In my opinion you would have greater success selling to the guy with a great suit collection."

"Agreed," Lindsay said, adding: "You mentioned you had a number of questions for the two entrepreneurs..."

"Yes. And my second question was: 'What are people buying that shows there is demand for this idea?' I then found that neither entrepreneur had done any real research. Both indicated they had no money for research. In one case the person was prepared to take out a home equity loan to fund the business, while the other was hoping to borrow money from friends and family to get started. So if you can't afford research, how do you find out what people are buying before risking your hard earned cash – and theirs – on a new venture?"

Lindsay shrugged. "I give up – how do you find out what people are buying?"

"Well, there are several free tools you can use to find out what people are looking for and are buying now. The first is to look at what people are searching for on the internet. You can use search term trackers at each of the major search engines to identify what people are looking for. Some of the best ones are Yahoo Buzz Index, MSN Search Insider and Google Zeitgeist. These will give you details on the most popular trends and ideas and tell you who's hot and who's not."

The StreetSmart Marketer finished his coffee, tossed the cardboard cup in a waste bin, and continued. "You can also use key word search software tools, of which there are many, to determine what terms people are searching for. Ones I like include Overture and Wordtracker. Another great resource is Amazon.com best seller list. This tells you what books people are buying in what categories. Most people like to read about subjects before buying or getting involved. E-bay is another great source of information on what people are both buying and selling. Also, every industry has its trade magazines and these can be a treasure trove of information. Any entrepreneur should subscribe to both the free ones and the paid ones if they intend to keep up with trends."

Lindsay nodded, clearly impressed. "That's a lot of very inexpensive ways to check out buying trends."

"There's more: If you can, it is always a good idea to buy your competitors' products or services. This will tell you, both; how they are selling what they sell and give you ideas about how what you offer might be able to improve on their weaknesses. It doesn't matter which of these low-cost research techniques you choose, but before launching a new product or idea, it is a good idea to learn about whether people are actively looking for a solution. If they are, then all you really have to do is find a way of tapping into this demand."

Lindsay smiled. "I really should be doing more of this market research myself. I often wonder what my customers are thinking when they use our services. I'd like to know what's going on in their head; what their customer experience is like..."

"A good way to get some insight in the area is to be your own customer."

"How do I do that?"

"I'll explain: There is a story that when Apple was developing its early products, Steve Jobs made sure he checked out the design of the packaging and the product himself before it ever went to customers. He felt that he needed to understand how a customer felt to receive and open what Apple was selling. Street-smart Marketers feel the same way about their customers and their business – they want to improve on the customer experience."

"That makes a lot of sense," Lindsay concurred.

"And here are several other simple things you can do to find out what it is like to be a customer of your organization: Call your firm, speak to sales, speak to customer service, and send an e-mail. Or, you can experience a sales presentation from one of your sales people, open the packaging, or if selling a service, experience the service in its entirety."

The StreetSmart Marketer paused a moment and removed a document from his jacket vest pocket.

"You should also check out your product or service and make a note of everything you need to change – and speaking of notes, here's a summary of the points we dealt with today," he added, handing Lindsay the folded document.

"Then," he continued, "you should implement the changes immediately. If you care about the experience and satisfaction of your customers, you have to know what they experience. Good marketing starts with an excellent product, not with a great story. And with that I must leave you to meet up with some friends..."

"Thank you so much, Mr. Hepworth," Lindsay said, waving goodbye as looked through the document. "As always, you've given me a wealth of information and useful advice – I can't wait to put it all into practice."

KEY 3:
Fix the Product or Service First

1. You can't expect marketing to save a "me too" product or service. You have to be the buyers' first choice. Firms with generic or deficient products or services must find ways to understand what their market niche wants; then find ways to make the offer more compelling to prospects.

2. Falling in love with your product can be dangerous to your wealth: Don't be blind to risks. If your product is untried, make sure it can find a market. Do market research.

3. Even if your idea is a good one, you're not going get far unless other people like it too and are willing to purchase or invest in making it happen. People vote with their cash.

4. Figure out what makes your business different or unique. Then, differentiate yourself from competitors. Advertising and marketing that's the same as everyone else's does as much for your competitors as it does for you. Marketing making the same claims as everyone else, forces customers to focus on one thing they do understand; price. This leads to an eroding of margins and a lack of customer loyalty.

5. Use key word search software tools such as Overture and Wordtracker to surf the Internet and find buyer trends.

6. Buy a competitor's products or services and then correct their flaws in your own product or service.

7. Become your own customer by opening your packaging and testing your products and services much like one of your customers. Then, improve/correct any flaws found.

4

"Our worst fear is not that we are inadequate. Our deepest fear is that we are powerful beyond measure. It is our light, not our darkness, that frightens us. We ask ourselves; who am I to be brilliant, gorgeous, talented or fabulous? Actually, who are you not to be? You are a child of God. Your playing small does not serve the world. And as we let our light shine, we unconsciously give other people permission to do the same. As we are liberated from our own fears our presence automatically liberates others."

- **Marianne Williamson** as quoted by Nelson Mandela in his inaugural address as president of South Africa.

KEY 4:
Sell the Bait First:

To catch ideal buyers you have to use the right bait. People are resistant to being sold, but if you can first offer something free that your prospects want you have a much better chance of engaging them and selling them something.

When Lindsay next caught up to the StreetSmart marketer he was seated on the park bench scribbling notes onto a steno pad. "Hello Mr. Hepworth," she smirked. "What's with the pen and notepad – are you mapping out today's discussion?"

Her playful commentary met with a smile. "Actually, Lindsay, I'm working out some ideas for an upcoming *StreetSmart Marketer* electronic newsletter."

"Oh," she smiled, "I've been meaning to tell you I'm a regular reader of your newsletter – it has an amazing amount of great advice from a number of sources and from well known marketing experts – including yourself of course."

"Of course," the StreetSmart Marketer grinned, as he put his notebook away. "I'm glad you find it useful."

Lindsay handed him his morning coffee as he rose from the bench and stretched.

"You don't have to get up – enjoy your coffee."

"It's such a nice day; I thought I might have my coffee while we took a walk through the park and talked. Are you up for that?"

"Sure," Lindsay confirmed. "What shall we talk about?"

"Well," he said, as they wandered along a wooded path, "why don't we continue our discussion about newsletters? In particular, I'd like to explain how newsletters can help you stay in touch and build deeper relationships with your customers and prospects."

"Sounds wonderful," Lindsay smiled. "I think newsletters are a great idea – we once had one at the print shop but it kind of fizzled out because everyone was too busy or didn't care enough to find good content and keep it going…"

"Unfortunately, that's a familiar story," the StreetSmart Marketer interjected. "Many business owners worry about how to stay in touch with a growing customer base. They know when you build relationships, you build sales. But they worry about the cost of person-to-person contact. One of the most common responses is to start a newsletter. Newsletters are an excellent medium to keep in touch with a large volume of customers and prospects. The idea works, but not everyone does a good job."

"That was certainly true in our case," Lindsay chuckled.

"The problem is; few people understand the few basic rules. It sounds a little obvious, but most newsletters are interesting to no one but the writer. If you talk about how wonderful your company, your new equipment or product is, you will be amazed how quickly people hit the delete button. Interesting newsletters are hard work and are written from the readers' point of view."

"That's easy to say," Lindsay objected, "but how can you possibly write about *your* company's new equipment from the *reader's* point of view?"

"Well, you can tell me how I can get what I need from you quicker, or cheaper or more simply. You can tell me that's why you bought the equipment. No one wants to know you have bought a new $500,000 printing press unless it translates into some specific advantage for them. You must speak to the readers' points of interest and get them thinking about how they can benefit from whatever it is you're writing about in your newsletter. It's better to focus on providing information to help your readers be more successful, or more informed – or show them how to avoid pitfalls in buying and using your type of products or services."

"Okay," Lindsay said quietly, "I can see that now, and I can understand how customers will relate, but I think people will still be turned off if your format is to just list advantages to them…"

"But you don't have to use that format all the time," the StreetSmart Marketer gently interjected. "People love quizzes and how-to guides. For example, as a printer, you could write about Seven Layout Secrets to Make Your Annual Reports More Effective. If you were in home improvements, you might write about Six Ideas For Giving Your Home Better Looks And Extra Living Space. Or if you were in carpet cleaning: Four Dangers Lurking In Your Carpets. That would be much more useful than talking about your 23 years of experience, your new trucks or the new guy you hired."

"Yes, it would be more useful," Lindsay agreed, "and more interesting too – I think I'd read a newsletter with the kinds of stories you just mentioned. And I would think photos and cartoons could add some interest as well."

"They certainly could – there are a number of layout elements and content formats you could employ to make your newsletter very attention-getting and interesting. You also need to make your newsletter newsworthy: People love to be kept up to date on interesting or important things going on in their business or industry – so make your newsletter a great source for news on industry developments."

"This is exciting – you've really inspired me!" Lindsay exclaimed. "I'm going to start up a new monthly newsletter and assign our best people blocks of time to provide research and content – I think this is really going to boost our customer relations."

"I like your enthusiasm – but be careful," the StreetSmart Marketer cautioned. "It's important that you produce a very effective newsletter that will attract and hold your customers' interest. Remember, it costs six times more to get a new customer than keep an old one. Don't send out a newsletter that will turn existing customers off. Make your newsletter interesting, newsy, entertaining and relevant to your readers. Make your customers look forward to each new issue."

"Absolutely," Lindsay grinned, as they neared a reedy duck pond. But her wide smile quickly faded. "Actually," she added hesitantly, "an engaging newsletter might help with another problem we've been having: People who indicate they'd like to use our services – but then end up turning us down..."

"Let's sit down for moment and discuss this," the StreetSmart Marketer invited. As they sat on the banks of the pond, he continued: "Lindsay, It's very true that many business people don't know what to do when a customer says no. Most entrepreneurs I know hate rejection and sometimes even take a customer turndown personally. But there is a way of creating a positive outcome from these situations."

Lindsay let out an unhappy sigh. "I'm listening."

"I believe one should do everything they possibly can to handle customer objections, but sometimes you simply have to accept that your customer is not going to buy. When this happens, there are two things you should always do to make the most of the situation. This strategy has provided me with incredible learning, and over time yielded a great deal of business from customers I might otherwise have lost."

With that, the StreetSmart Marketer stopped talking, placed a blade of grass in his mouth and stared at the blue summer sky.

Lindsay found herself smiling again as she gave him a playful shove. "You can stop teasing and share your strategy any time now," she laughingly admonished him.

"I shall – and, I might add, it's nice to see that smile back again. Now, where was I. Oh yes, the strategy: The first thing: When a customer says "no" to your sales pitch, ask her why. Then listen carefully and respectfully to her answer. Take notes. This information is likely to contain the clues you need to improve your offer. Thank her again and tell her you won't bother her until you have something better to offer her. Then, when you do have something better, give her a call. She will probably accept it since you've proven to be polite and useful – and she may very well be ready for a change by the time you do have something good to offer her."

"That's very insightful, very helpful advice," Lindsay said appreciatively. "And the second thing?"

"The second thing is that you should also make sure that your customer's details are in your database, and begin to nurture the relationship. If you know what her interests are, or what challenges she is facing, you can send relevant articles from time to time. If you have a newsletter, make sure she is on your list of recipients. If you have any customer events make sure she is on the invitation list. This information should be of real value to her – not just a sales pitch to sell your wares. Only by constantly delivering value can you show her that you should be top of her list the next time she is looking for your kind of products or services."

The two continued chatting as a mother duck floated by on the pond with seven ducklings lined up behind her. A gentle breeze rustled the leaves of a nearby willow and prompted an array of birds to take flight as a squirrel ran chattering by.

"You know," Lindsay confided, "in all the time I've worked so close by this park, this is the first time I've really seen this much of it – it's absolutely lovely."

"I agree – it's a great place to clear my head of distractions and collect my thoughts. Have you been to its petting zoo?"

"No – but that sounds like fun."

"We should have enough time – and we can discuss more marketing approaches along the way." With that, the two friends leisurely strolled towards the distant sounds of sheep and goats.

"You know, Lindsay," the StreetSmart Marketer began, "the newsletters we've been discussing are really part of a broader theme: that of giving customers and prospects something free of value to them. To catch ideal buyers you have to use the right bait. People are resistant to being sold, but if you can first offer something free that your prospects want, you have a much better chance of engaging them and selling them something."

As Lindsay nodded her agreement, he continued. "A key question you should ask yourself is this: Are you a *giver* company or a *taker* company? As a StreetSmart Marketer, you know there are giver companies and there are taker companies, just like there are people who are givers and there are people who are takers. We are attracted to people and to companies who are givers, so it is a good idea to build this into the way you market."

"I guess we do a little of that on an informal basis," Lindsay considered. "Our sales people tend to give small discounts and free pens to help make a purchase happen."

"Almost all of us give away small amounts during the steps that lead up to the sale," the StreetSmart Marketer agreed. "But I am suggesting that you give away things as part of your strategy. It is easier to get to hard-to reach prospects this way. People are more likely to refer you if they know that you will give something away to the person they are referring you to, and people feel the need for reciprocity when you give them something. This eventually makes them easier to sell to."

"So, it's more effective to give away more substantial things and on a consistent, built-in basis to attract sales," Lindsay mused.

"Yes, that's very true," the StreetSmart Marketer confirmed. "So, consider what you might be able to give away for free. Depending on the business you are in, you could give free initial consultations, free training, free samples, demonstrations, seminars and executive briefings. What under-utilized assets do you have that could be used to build better relationships rather than lying around being ignored and unused?"

"I'll have to think about that – but can you give me an example of unused or under-utilized assets?"

"Sure; in one of my businesses we had a large database of accumulated research results from hundreds of studies. We used this information to compare new survey results against the database, but did little else with it. However, one day we analyzed the database, and identified some startling trends. We produced a report for customers and prospects and used the findings for numerous free activities including briefings, presentations and seminars. This tool probably was responsible for creating more opportunities than almost any other marketing item we produced."

"That's one handy, effective tool," Lindsay acknowledged, clearly impressed. "But I'm wondering how to go about this."

In response, the StreetSmart Marketer tore some blank pages from his notepad and gestured for Lindsay to sit down on a park bench opposite the petting zoo. "Please be seated," he invited her, "and here's a pen. I'd like you to write down what you can give away to build relationships with your prospects and clients. With existing clients a surprise bonus often does wonders for your relationship, so don't ignore this. Be generous, you will find a strong correlation between what you give and what you get. As Jay Abraham, North America's Grand Master of Marketing says; 'The most self-serving thing you can do in business, is to give selflessly,' and I believe there's a great deal of truth in that."

"I've jotted down free consultations, free samples and free seminars already – and I'm sure I can think of a few more."

"I'm sure these valuable gifts will make a difference. They all fall under the low-cost entrepreneurial marketing approach we discussed a while ago. A lot of this comes down to finding and utilizing the most effective methods and approaches to get your message out, while bypassing some of the less effective, costly and traditional marketing methods. I'm not sure who first said this, but it's very true that: 'When information is abundant, attention is scarce'. And it's certainly true when it comes to marketing. As mentioned during one our earlier meetings, people are bombarded with marketing messages. This means if you want to make appointments with decision-makers and get heard, you need to develop superior access vehicles. Telephone prospecting, using the same old type of messages won't cut it, nor will the traditional one page introductory letter accompanied by a brochure."

"What *should* we do?" Lindsay asked.

"We have to find ways of delivering value before people will pay attention. One way to do this is to invite your prospects to participate in an event where they will learn something that will make them more successful. For example, one of our clients was selling safety equipment to firms that seemed more interested in price. Our client's goal was to access people in the firm *above* the level of the buying department, who would then set the criteria for the buying department."

"How would they go about doing that?" Lindsay inquired. "It doesn't sound like an easy thing to do – the people higher up in a company aren't always easy to reach."

"That's very true; it's not usually an easy task. Unfortunately, it is almost impossible to attract senior people's attention unless there has been a recent incident to make them aware of a need to do something. If you contact senior people on a subject like that, you almost certainly will be referred elsewhere in the organization, or worse, be completely ignored. So you might offer to run an executive briefing on *The 4 Most Common Lawsuits Arising From On The Job Injuries And What To Do To Avoid Them.*
He paused, then said: "You might be able to get the VP of HR to attend and also the CFO. This would be a lot easier to sell than safety equipment, but by raising awareness at the highest levels of the need for safety equipment it's likely the safety equipment company would make some sales in the weeks following the briefing. How could you apply this principle to your business?"

"In our case, a seminar presented to purchasing agents as well as the highest ranking people at a company would likely work best," Lindsay mused. "We'd play up the fact that you can get discounts for multiple jobs and for getting files in to us early on."

"Another superior access vehicle might be to run a round table discussion with a number of your target prospective clients discussing something that is keeping them awake at night."

"Can you give me an example of this?" Lindsay asked.

"Sure, imagine if you wanted to sell your services to investment bankers, you could run a meeting with a number of CEOs from rapid growth firms to discuss: *How To Raise Money In A Tight Market. Best Practices and New Insights.* You could probably fairly easily get a number of CEOs to attend."

"I wouldn't think getting CEOs involved would be a problem with such an interesting meeting topic," Lindsay agreed.

"Once you have the CEOs' attendance confirmed; it's a simple matter of getting a few targeted investment bankers to participate. And once the bankers participate in an activity of this nature, dialog becomes easy, as does the opportunity to build a relationship. If you don't want to do this, there are firms you can hire that specialize in running these kinds of meetings. In summary, if you find you can't access the people you need to reach to get decisions, you have to create a superior access vehicle that will open the doors to the people you need to meet. Be creative – ask yourself: what information do they need and how can you deliver it?"

The two companions now wandered into the petting zoo where they fed quarters into converted gumball machines to get handfuls of feed for eager goats crowding around them. One goat was most interested in chewing on Lindsay's floral dress, but after a bit of coaxing he opted for the purchased feed instead.

After a few more moments with these four-footed characters, Lindsay and the StreetSmart Marketer began walking back to their usual meeting place.

As they passed the duck pond, Lindsay had a thought: "I think everything we've discussed today, once put in practice, will also help earn me some referrals – but is there anything else I could or should be doing to build that referrals list.

The StreetSmart Marketer paused a moment and then replied: "One effective way to get unsolicited referrals is by 'wowing' your customers. There is no question that businesses that wow their customers grow quicker than firms that do not. But how do you wow your customers consistently? This is a question that should be top of mind for every business owner. Many people believe you 'wow' customers by exceeding expectations every time they come in contact with your firm. While I believe this to be true for the most part, and is an excellent goal, in reality I think it is somewhat simplistic and not entirely practical. For example how do you 'wow' a customer when you are sending an invoice, or asking them about a late payment of a bill?"

"Good point," Lindsay concurred.

"So many businesses fail even on handling base expectations. How often do we leave voice mails for suppliers that take days to be returned or send e-mails that never get responded to? I believe that there are simple standards that you can hold everyone in your firm accountable for. For example, one fellow I know, Adam, has an electronics business that requires his staff to work in people's homes. He trains his staff to adhere strictly to four standards, which few of his competitors adhere to. Almost all of his business comes from referrals and he believes these behaviours are at the root of this revenue."

"What are the behaviours?"

"Well, the first is to show up on time. His work teams make appointments and work hard to leave early enough to show up at another customer's house at the appointed time. He believes this commitment to a specific time is rare in his business and it shows reliability, something also generally lacking in the world of contractors."

"That's for sure – I can't believe the number of people we make appointments with who show up 30 minutes late with no explanation or apology."

"The second behaviour is to say please and thank you. While this seems trivial, Adam believes that this shows respect for the other party and builds rapport between worker and client. He also believes that good manners are rare these days and make his people stand out."

"Politeness seems to be a lost art for too many people."

"He also insists that his workers do what they say they will. Not following through is grounds for dismissal. Doing what you say you will shows consistency, reliability and trustworthiness."

"Reliability – another lost art," Lindsay observed.

"Finally, his workers are never allowed to leave their work unfinished without explanation. Even where installations take weeks there is communication with the client about progress and when the workers will be back. It's no more complex than that – everyone knows the standards to be met and agrees to adhere to them. This approach results in great communication between supplier and client, high levels of trust and satisfaction – and the referrals come in almost daily."

"What's the best way to get referrals?" Lindsay asked.

"You should ask for them – but also earn them. Asking for referrals is an ongoing process, an essential element of what you do to grow your business. As such it should be an integral component of all of your dealings with clients. In your early discussions with new customers, let them know that it's your normal practice to look for referrals from satisfied clients. They might even be in a position to make referrals at that preliminary stage of the relationship. At the very least, this will prepare them for your asking for referrals from time to time. Ideal times to ask for referrals are on completion of different stages of work or on receipt of a compliment from a client. To encourage referrals: tell your clients how much you enjoy doing business with them; acknowledge that they probably know similar people; since they know the type of people you prefer to work with, you are offering them the opportunity to tell their friends and associates how they have benefited from working with you. Offer referrals incentives such as thank you gifts or discounts on their next purchase.

"We've talked before about networking," Lindsay observed, "but I'm finding our networking isn't bringing us much sales."

"One thing you need to understand is the difference between networking and selling. Having a good network is a vital resource for any business person. For many people networking is their main source of business. Yet most people get little benefit from their efforts. They attend networking events and collect lots of business cards from people who aren't qualified prospects. This feels like progress, perhaps it feels like work, but unless these contacts are likely to become prospects it's largely a waste of time."

He paused, then continued. "This kind of networking yields modest results and is usually cover for a broken or non-existent marketing process. To network effectively you have to fish where the fish are. Where are you likely to meet prospects for your business? What do you want them to do? Once you know the answer to these questions focus your attention on relevant venues where you can find people who can move you toward your goals. Networking is far more passive and does not generally put bread on the table. Selling is understanding people's problems and offering them a solution that they will pay you for."

The two had now reached their usual meeting place. The StreetSmart Marketer reached in his vest pocket and removed a summary of much of what they had discussed.

Lindsay accepted the summary with a smile. "Once again you've given me a welcome escape from the office chaos and great advice for taming the turmoil when I return to it. I don't know how to thank you..."

"Your success is thanks enough for me – we'll meet again next week; same time; same place."

KEY 4:
Sell the Bait first

1. Interesting and effective newsletters are hard work and are written from the readers' point of view and must not be self-serving.

2. When a customer says "no" to your sales pitch, ask her why. Then listen carefully and respectfully to her answer. Take notes. This information is likely to contain the clues you need to improve your offer. Get back in touch once your offer has been improved.

3. Make sure your customer's details are in your database, and begin to nurture the relationship. If you know what her interests are, or what challenges she is facing, you can send relevant articles from time to time. Send her your newsletter and other information of value to build trust.

4. To catch ideal buyers you have to use the right bait. People are resistant to being sold, but if you can first offer something free that your prospects want, you have a better chance of engaging them and selling them something.

5. Find ways of delivering value to get people's attention, such as inviting prospects to an event where they'll learn something that will make them more successful.

6. Wow your customers with polite, friendly professional service that will make them want to choose you over competitors.

7. Ask for referrals but also earn by doing a great job that the client appreciates so he'll recommend your services.

8. Understand the difference between networking and sales; then practice effective networking to build future sales.

5

"The majority of men meet with failure because of their lack of persistence in creating new plans to take the place of those which fail."
- **Napoleon Hill**

KEY 5:
Wooing Prospects:

Marketing, like dating, shouldn't be rushed. Marketers who ask for too big a commitment early on run the risk of frightening otherwise interested parties. Advertisers who try to make a sale without a full description of the offer risk losing customers that don't see the value of what's being offered.

The StreetSmart Marketer watched Lindsay approach the park bench with a spring in her step and a smile on her face.

"Hello Lindsay, you're looking... younger."

Lindsay laughed. "You're the second person to say that today. I have to say I feel younger, and when I look in the mirror, I think I look younger too. I think all the stress I'd been under was making me feel – and look – much older than I am."

"I've been meaning to ask you, how is your father?"

"Much better, thanks. He's recovering at home now and he seems back to his old self again. But the doctors are insisting he continue to take it easy for a while before going back to work."

"He must be very proud of the progress you're making."

"Actually, he doesn't know anything about it yet. The doctors have advised keeping him as free from stress as possible right now so any shop talk is strictly off limits until he's ready to go back."

"Even though the news is all good at the print shop?"

"I'm afraid so... but, to be honest, the news isn't all good."

"Oh?"

"Don't get me wrong; we've made wonderful progress by putting your advice to work. Sales and revenue are up and most of the feedback from customers is pretty positive, but..."

"But?"

"But there's this one keen salesman with an eager beaver, aggressive sales approach. It's great that he's really promoting and pushing our services so hard, but a lot of the customers don't seem to... like him very much. Some of them avoid him or think of excuses to cut their meeting short..."

"It sounds like he needs to romance your customers by making the easy sale first and then nurturing them with helpful information until they are ready to buy. Since wooing prospects is the subject of our key lesson today, I'll be happy to elaborate."

"Please do," Lindsay said, adding "and before I forget, here's your coffee, still nice and hot."

"Thanks," the StreetSmart Marketer replied, taking a sip. "Now, I'll give you idea of what I'm getting at: When I was a teenager, I had a friend Gavin, who had a very direct approach with the young ladies in the town where we lived. We used to laugh because he got a lot of slaps, and we were also envious because he was sometimes successful."

"Quite the little charmer," Lindsay quipped sarcastically.

"Thinking back, I realize that one of the reasons Gavin got slapped so often, is that he was trying to make a very difficult sale. He tended to fail more often than he succeeded. He just didn't know how to romance his prospects."

"Sounds like he was trying to rush into things too fast, without thinking about how the girls felt," Lindsay suggested.

"That's very true. Now, ask yourself, when dealing with your customers, is your sale rep trying to close a sale that is hard to make? If you are advertising or selling to people who have never heard of you and you start off right away asking for a relatively big commitment like asking for an hour of their time for a meeting, the answer is almost certainly no. It is also true when trying to sell big ticket items or fairly complex solutions to new prospects. Is your eager sales rep making the same mistake as Gavin and turning off prospects, simply because they're not ready for such a big step?"

"That may well be the problem," Lindsay mused thoughtfully.

"As marketers, we can't afford to undermine our efforts with this kind of mistake. To reach a qualified prospect and get turned down because you are moving too quickly is simply too expensive, and the opportunity cost is too high. Like most marketing mistakes, the issues are subtle and are not always obvious to the casual observer."

"I know we sure can't afford to lose prospects," Lindsay concurred. "I'll talk to the rep and get him to alter his approach."

"The key with marketing is to understand that no matter how much success you have with a program, you owe it to yourself to continually find ways to improve your results. It costs exactly the same amount to run a direct mail piece, a sales campaign or an advertisement that yields 2 per cent, 3 per cent or 4 per cent, so why be content with any response rate, let alone a modest one? What's more, you can often get dramatic increases with only very minor changes that cost nothing."

"What kind of changes do you have in mind?" Lindsay asked.

"Well, I have found the easiest way to increase your success rate with customers, is to get a little romance going. The key is to make the easy sale first. My young friend might have been more successful if he had built trust by inviting his prospects for coffee, getting to know them a little better and understanding what they were wanting out of a relationship. So it is with your customers. You have to be prepared to invest some time and energy in building trust."

"How would we go about making the easy sale first?"

"First, making the easy sale first usually involves offering something free. Let the customer try out your services at no risk. So, what can you offer for free without breaking the bank? The simplest gift is information. Do you have information that is useful and valuable to your prospective customers? It must not be self-serving, otherwise it defeats the purpose. The best kind of information is the kind that helps the customer avoid making bad buying decisions, or protects them from dangers they might not even be aware of."

The StreetSmart Marketer took a long sip of coffee and then continued. "You can also offer a free, no obligation consultation or service to new prospects. If your services are good and your prospects are properly qualified, the downside risk is minimal for you. You should get a lot more people trying your service and becoming customers. Remember, I did say, make the easy sale first. You still have to sell, but it will be easier. Be clear about the benefits your prospects will get if they take this first step. Don't assume though that because you are offering something free, people will automatically take you up on your offer. However, once they do take you up on your offer, you are well on your way to developing a profitable relationship."

Lindsay nodded her head in agreement. "I think I'll discuss this approach with the sales rep – it may be a very good way for him to start tailoring his whole approach to really focus on the customer's needs rather than simply pumping our product."

"Good idea," the StreetSmart Marketer concurred. "And while you're assessing this situation with the sales rep, try to determine if he's prone to blaming your prospects when products or services are not selling as well as he'd like."

"I hope that's not a problem, but I'll certainly check into it. Do many professional sales people actually blame the prospect for not buying?"

"Unfortunately, that can and does happen among frustrated sales people. This kind of attitude is not unique to high-tech firms, but it was definitely a dominant theme recently when I was a guest at a discussion group for technology companies selling into the health care industry. There was a fascinating discussion about what is happening in health care and how technology is changing the landscape in this rapidly changing environment. Yet, despite these great opportunities, there was a lot of discussion of how prospects in this industry don't really understand what is being offered by technology firms. There was also much complaining about the un-willingness of prospects to take risks. In general, it sounded like the customers were to blame for a lot of the problems these firms were experiencing..."

"What an attitude!" Lindsay exclaimed in disgust.

"It sounded to me like many of these firms had it backwards. They'd fallen in love with the products instead of their customers. It's not your customers' responsibility to understand what you sell and how it could help them; it's yours. This is one of the most fundamental principles of marketing. These firms clearly didn't understand their customers' needs as well as they should, and as a result, blamed the customers when the sales didn't materialize."

"As you've said, it's important to focus on customer needs."

"Exactly, the only way to sell is to start from the prospect's side. If you don't, you'll generally get the same result as these unfortunate firms. Starting from the prospect's side means you can't pitch a solution simply because you think it is a good idea. Nor should you talk about how wonderful you or your products are. No one cares and there are hundreds of firms offering the same undifferentiated 'stuff' you do."

"No one likes to listen to someone bragging," Lindsay agreed.

"That's right; you have to stop talking about yourself. We've all been trapped by bragging people like this at social events. In that environment it may be difficult for you to get away, but not so for the sales prospects – they will just ignore you. You have to remember, no one wants to be sold, so you have to approach it from the perspective of serving the customer. A good mindset is 'You Matter. Your well being is important to me. Let me see how I can help.' This mindset forces you to focus on the customer first and for your firm to become the champion of your customers and prospects; ultimately making certain you are their most trusted supplier, because you leave them in a better condition than when you started. From this position it is much easier to gain acceptance of your ideas."

"How do you begin this process?"

"The first step is to convince your prospects to give you their attention. The only way you can do this is if your marketing messages speak to their desires, frustrations and fears. You must convince them you're worth spending time with or your website is worth visiting. You have to be different than your competitors. If you are saying essentially the same thing, you're indistinguishable in the crowd. A good headline for a letter, brochure or web site is a good start... but it is not enough. You have to have substance that will keep them involved with you, either reading your letters, listening to your suggestions or reading what's on your web site."

"So, combining attention-getting presentation with content?"

"Yes, you can only make this work if you provide value. It's not enough that you have a great product or service; you need to show them how you can help them solve a problem. Good products are a table stake in business and bad products don't stay around very long. The moment prospects no longer perceive value, you lose them. There are too many competing messages out there, to expect them to listen to you any longer than it takes them to decide you are worth listening to, or to cut and run."

"Can testimonials add value to the message content?"

"Testimonials are critical for both products and services. Social proof is very effective in encouraging undecided people to move forward. Few people want to be pioneers unless the risk is very low. The newer the product, the greater the perceived risk.
You have to find ways to remove the risk – and we'll talk more about that at our next meeting – because if you can't remove the risk, you may have a great product or service that never sees the light of day. It may even be necessary to work free on occasion in

exchange for testimonials, if what you have is unproven. Think of it as a marketing cost."

"Prospects must believe I'll meet their needs," Lindsay noted.

"You also have to convince prospects that what you offer is at least good value, but better still a bargain. You do this by making dramatic comparisons with the current situation and presenting this information in a compelling way."

"Finally," he added, handing Lindsay a summary of their discussion, "you have to make it very easy for them to buy. You can do this with extended payment terms, time-limited offers, guarantees and other incentives. Only when you demonstrate in believable ways that you have your prospects' interests at heart and you're intent on helping them make the right decision, will you reduce the resistance to your products and services."

"You've provided a wealth of material I'll be discussing with our sales rep," Lindsay beamed. "I'm sure he'll be receptive to all of it as he's been genuinely perplexed at why he's not getting more sales and he's looking for answers – answers you've just provided."

"Lindsay," the StreetSmart Marketer smiled as he rose from the bench, "on that note, I must be going – I have to prepare for a seminar I'm giving this evening."

Lindsay watched her friend leave until he was a distant speck on the horizon. Then she rose from the bench, smoothed the creases in her jacket, and began to leisurely walk back to her office.

KEY 5:
Wooing Prospects

1. Marketing, like dating, shouldn't be rushed. Marketers who ask for too big a commitment early on risk frightening otherwise interested parties. Advertisers who try to make a sale without a full description of the offer risk losing customers that don't see the value of what's being offered.

2. The key with marketing is to understand that no matter how much success you have with a program, you owe it to yourself to continually find ways to improve your results. You can often get dramatic increases with only very minor changes that cost nothing."

3. Making the easy sale first usually involves offering something free. Let the customer try out your services at no risk. So, what can you offer for free without breaking the bank? The simplest gift is information. The best kind of information is the kind that helps the customer avoid making bad buying decisions, or protects them from dangers they might not even be aware of. After that you should stay in touch and nurture the relationship with further value-added information as you move towards making the sale.

4. It's not enough to have a great product or service; you need to show clients you can help them solve a problem.

5. Stop talking about yourself and listen to the customer. Don't fall in love with your product – fall in love with your customer instead. Meeting their needs means sales.

6. Testimonials are critical for new products and services. Social proof is very effective in encouraging undecided people to move forward.

7. Use extended payment terms, guarantees, time-limited offers and other incentives. Make it easy for clients to buy.

6

"Goods satisfactory or money refunded"
- **Timothy Eaton**, whose famous phrase over 120 years ago
revolutionized Canadian business.

KEY 6:
Risk Reversal:

Risk causes hesitation, and hesitation kills sales, so shoulder the risk. Guarantees are one of the most effective ways of doing this, but you have to put them out front so people know you stand by what you are selling.

As he watched Lindsay cross the street with their coffees and head to the park, the StreetSmart Marketer discerned a troubled look on the young woman's face.

"Ah," he smiled on being handed a coffee, "smells wonderful and it's nice and hot – I'll enjoy this. Now, tell me Lindsay, what accounts for your worried expression on such a beautiful day?"

"Oh, nothing, really," Lindsay replied awkwardly.

"I don't believe that for a moment – tell me what's wrong," the StreetSmart Marketer said soothingly before taking a sip.

"Well... alright. The sales rep and I talked and he's using most of the tips you provided at our last meeting – focusing on the needs of the customer, using testimonials, providing fee consultations and information of value to the client, making the easy sale first, making it easy to buy – everything, and it's really made a positive difference, except..."

Lindsay took a sip of her coffee and continued. "Except that even with his new and improved behaviour, some of the newest prospects just can't seem to commit to buying... it's as though they don't have enough trust in us to make a purchase..."

"This problem relates well to the subject of today's key lesson," the StreetSmart Marketer interjected. "Bringing in new customers is expensive and often difficult. Here is one effective but frequently overlooked way to reduce the difficulty: Reverse the risk. Businesses, even the most customer-oriented ones, tend to expect the customer to take the risk when doing business with them. The premise is almost: 'We have great products, so you can try them if you pay us first,' as opposed to; 'We have great products and we believe in them so much, that if they don't do exactly what they're supposed to, we don't want you to pay." Guaranteeing results is a sure-fire way to attract new customers. And the stronger your guarantee, the better. The difference in attitude is subtle, but will have a huge impact on your customers' readiness to do business with you."

"How so?"

"For a new business or a new relationship, the first, traditional stance – that of requiring the customer to pay first – makes the sale much more difficult. Trust is one of the most important ingredients in any sale. Business is all about trust. Peddle all the features and benefits you want, but people will seldom part with money until trust is there. But building trust takes time – and hesitation kills businesses. So do away with dithering by reversing the risk."

The StreetSmart Marketer paused to drink his coffee, then continued. "One way to build trust and credibility quickly is to reverse the risk. As a business, you can make an explicit offer to take the risk when a customer buys your product and thereby increase sales very quickly. Some examples of ways you can do this include offering an unconditional full money back guarantee, if certain results are not achieved. Or, if you can afford it, you can agree not to deposit the customer's cheque for 30 days, until the customer has had the opportunity to try your product or service. You can also offer a better-than-risk-free guarantee. Offer the customer gifts for trying the product or service. If they are dissatisfied in any way, not only will you refund their money but they also get to keep the gifts, simply for trying your offer."

"We already informally give refunds if there's a problem…"
"Exactly, most of us would refund an unhappy customer's money without hesitation; why not make it an explicit benefit of your offer up front? Build it into your advertising, direct response and sales pitches. Just make your offer as powerful as possible. A 60-day guarantee is good, but a one-year guarantee is better, as it

offers buyers more value while also reducing the deadline pressure to return the product. Make your guarantee obvious, instead of casually mentioning it or only offering when necessary. Doing this will build trust and encourage trial and increase sales."

"Won't some customers take advantage of us?"

"Sure, some will take advantage, but the majority won't, and the risk reversal will increase significantly the number of buyers willing to try your service. Think of those that abuse you as a promotional cost and you won't regret it. Yes, I know someone who complained to Sears about a table they bought 15 years earlier. They ended up getting a full refund. But now they won't shop anywhere else, so even that deal benefited Sears in the end. My experience is that sincerity and creativity can satisfy most customers' problems – and help retain clients who might have otherwise been lost. Most people won't abuse your trust. You'll find the advantages quickly outweigh the disadvantages."

"How should we frame the terms of our guarantee?"

"You have to make your guarantee powerful and appealing – the more outrageous the better. I prefer to offer a better than money back guarantee, where the customer gets to keep something of value, simply for trying the product or service, regardless if they keep the product or not. Customers should pay for your products and services, but you have got to make it easy for them to buy. This is one very effective way of doing it. Offer customers a gift for trying your product or service. If they are dissatisfied, they will receive a full refund, but they also get to keep the gift."

"I really like this approach – despite it being a little risky – and I can see it helping to build our business," Lindsay considered.

"However, the risk is very small versus the potential gain. Look at it this way: You're offering good quality product and services. Your job is to attract customers' attention and build trust. So break out of the timidity trap. Stand behind your product and watch the customers take note."

"And they will take note," Lindsay agreed. "I know that as a customer myself, I much prefer to shop at stores that offer money-back unconditional guarantees."

"The retail experience is an excellent example of guarantees at work as a means of building trust and encouraging purchases. Timothy Eaton and his Eaton stores got it right over 120 years ago when they pledged: 'Goods satisfactory or money refunded' and in so doing, revolutionized Canadian retail business. At a time when the consumer's only protection was 'buyer beware' and guarantees for the most part did not exist, Eaton took the risk out of shopping at his stores by taking responsibility for the consequences. Many retailers today still promote money-back guarantees. But few other businesses do. And that's a key reason they find it so expensive to attract new clients: They make customers assume the risks of doing business with them."

"The key seems to be; boldly stating a guarantee that you're probably already quietly offering anyway," Lindsay contemplated.

"Sure, why keep your guarantee a secret when it's such a sales-getter. And a bold statement can work wonders: A friend of mine, who wrote a book on sales techniques, made this offer on the last page: 'If after applying the concepts in his book some readers don't see a substantial increase in sales, they can return the book to him personally for a no-questions-asked refund.' That guarantee pretty much eliminates customer hesitation. It also shows what great confidence the author has in his product. Better still, he says, no one has ever returned a copy of the book. If you qualify your guarantee in this manner – making the application of the concepts a criteria to qualify for a refund – you will also discourage those troublemakers who haven't even given your product a chance."

"I like the sound of that," Lindsay smiled, "but I don't think we could apply that kind of try-it-first approach to our guarantees."

"You really don't need to," the StreetSmart Marketer noted. "I've run a number of companies, from consulting to human-resource development, and I have always offered a money-back guarantee. I believe this has boosted my sales significantly. It gives me an advantage over less confident-seeming competitors, and it's a great deal-closer. Yet I have never had to pay out a penny.

That doesn't mean no one ever calls me on my guarantee. I have had to handle a few customer complaints. But here's the other benefit of a guarantee: it encourages unhappy customers to contact you. Instead of walking away – and possibly bad-mouthing your product to future prospects – unhappy customers call and explain their problem – giving you an opportunity to fix things."

"That's a great advantage I hadn't thought of," Lindsay said.

"Another very successful way to build sales is to use service to open doors to new prospects."

"That sounds interesting."

"It is, and I have an example in mind that I'm sure you as a printer, can relate to: Kim Armstrong has a successful screen printing business. She focuses on large national firms that buy screen printing in big volumes. Her business has slowed considerably over the last three years and her biggest challenge has been getting targeted new prospects to see her. These big companies get countless calls everyday from hopeful sales people intent on selling their firm's screen printing services. While Kim is fun to talk to, does great work at reasonable prices and is very service-oriented, these benefits don't open as many doors as they used to. The problem: everyone is selling, but no one wants to be sold. However, by changing her approach from selling to *serving*, she now gets in to see people she'd been unable to reach before."

"How has she managed to do that?"

"Well, over the last month or two Kim has been gathering information on how to get better results from their screen-printing. She has been looking at ways to save money, finding out how to make sure that the images she prints are more effective in the market and uncovering new developments in the field. Kim's approach has been to offer this information to prospects whether they use her services or not. She recently developed a booklet called *25 Ways To Save Money And Profit More From Your*

Screen Printing. Her approach is now to position herself as a Screen Printing Consultant and to call prospects to tell them about this free booklet. She sells them on why it will be useful to them and suggests she deliver it in person."

"Clever," Lindsay said softly in admiration.

"Her whole focus is on serving and helping the customer. She acknowledges her long term goal is to do business with the firm, but that she is doing this service for them without obligation. She has more than doubled her strike rate in getting appointments, and is now getting business from the firms she has targeted, instead of waiting for business to come from its traditional sources."

"Amazing," Lindsay smiled. "I'm sure our print shop could help our customers in a similar manner, offering services without obligation in the likelihood those firms that we help will want to do business with us at some point. That's a great approach to building a business – thank you so much for sharing it with me."

The StreetSmart Marketer smiled back. "On that note, we should part paths," he said, handing her a summary of the day's discussion. "I'll have to leave now if I'm to make an important conference call at my office – we'll meet here again next week."

As the two went their separate ways, Lindsay realized she had never felt so happy or confident when facing business challenges.

KEY 6:
Risk Reversal

1. Realize that risk causes hesitation, and hesitation kills sales, so shoulder the risk. Guarantees are one of the most effective ways of doing this, but you have to put them out front so people know you stand by what you are selling.

2. One way to reverse the risk is to offer an unconditional money back guarantee, if certain results are not achieved.

3. If you already offer an informal guarantee, why not build it into your marketing program to build trust and sales?

4. Most people will not abuse a guarantee and it's a very effective way of securing customer loyalty.

5. Offer customers a gift for trying your product or service. If they are dissatisfied, they will receive a full refund, but they also get to keep the gift.

6. A guarantee encourages unhappy customers to contact you. Instead of bad-mouthing your product, unhappy customers call and explain their problem – giving you an opportunity to fix things.

7. Changing your focus from selling to serving customers can make difference in building your client base later on.

7

"Employ your time in improving yourself by other men's writings, so that you shall gain easily what others have laboured hard for."
- Socrates

"Never forget that only dead fish swim with the stream"
-Unknown

KEY 7:
Creating effective advertising:

Simply changing a headline has been shown to double or triple response rates and in some cases improve response rates by up to 21 times.

The StreetSmart Marketer was seated comfortably on the park bench, reading his newspaper and waiting for Lindsay. As he absent-mindedly reached for a phantom coffee, a real cup of coffee was deftly placed in his hand. He looked up from his paper to see Lindsay standing before him.

"How's that for service?" she asked with a grin. "Sorry I'm a little late, but I was delayed at the office trying to work out an advertising problem."

"Anything I can help you with?"

"I don't know; we do a bit of advertising in publications read by our customers, but it doesn't seem to lead to more business."

"So you'd like to know how to make your advertising more effective and how to generate more leads from your advertising?"

"In a nutshell, yes."

"Interestingly enough, our topic today is on advertising – we'll be discussing the seventh key: recognizing that image advertising is for big business... and of course also recognizing what advertising approaches work best for smaller businesses."

Lindsay flashed a smile. "I gather we're already starting."

"Sure, why not? Let me start by saying marketing for small business isn't a beauty contest. You should really run only direct response, not image advertising. Direct response is 100 per cent measurable and if done properly, you get the image advertising free. I received a call the other day from a consultant, whose specialty is improving the performance of corporate websites. He told me he had been advertising his services in two magazines and that the results had been disappointing to say the least. He wanted to know how to generate more leads from his advertising."

"My problem exactly," Lindsay noted. "How did you help?"

"To understand his situation better, I asked some questions. My first question seemed to make him uncomfortable. I asked him if there is a market for his services. After a moment, he regained his composure and began to assure me there was a very viable market for his services. If this is the case, then why was he having trouble selling his services? He seemed to be advertising in the right places."

The StreetSmart Marketer took a long drink of coffee and then continued. "After several more questions, I think I discovered the reason his ads weren't working. I think it is the main reason why so many ads don't work well: They simply do not give the reader a reason to read further, and they turn off the reader because the copy is all about the advertiser and not about the reader. In this case, the web consultant's ad began with his very attractive three-colour corporate logo and the headline 'Web Improvement Consulting,' followed by a description of his experience and why he was so good at what he does."

"But nothing about why the reader should care?"

"Correct – StreetSmart Marketers avoid the two fundamental mistakes made here: assuming their readers understand the need, and not offering their readers any reason to read on. The bold prominence of our consultant's three-colour logo added nothing except cost, as he is a new unknown brand. If you must have your logo on your advertising, place it towards the bottom with your contact information. StreetSmart Marketers know the reader is not interested in who you are until she is interested in your offer."

"Good point."

"I then asked the consultant: 'If owners of websites have been surviving without your services, what would make a website owner read this ad?' He told me he could show almost every website owner how to generate more traffic by understanding a few key principles and making simple changes to the site to reflect these principles. He knew that – but his prospects don't even know they have a problem, so why would they seek his help?"

"Good question – how did you deal with it?"

"One of the key things you want to do is to develop a powerful headline to make sure your copy is read – and in this case, I suggested a different headline, that would encourage the reader to at least read the next sentence. The headline I suggested was: 'How Four Common Mistakes Can Make Your Website Up To 45% Less Effective as a Lead Generator.' Readers may not know if they need a web consultant, but they would almost certainly be interested in finding out if something they are doing is sabotaging their efforts to produce business. Thus, I also suggested a sub-heading describing an under-performing website, so readers could relate to what he had to tell them."

"I know that headline would make me want to read more," Lindsay acknowledged. "That must have made a big difference."

The StreetSmart Marketer paused for a gulp of coffee, then resumed. "I believe having read the headline, there was a greater chance readers would read the sub-head that followed. Simply changing a headline has been shown to double or triple response rates and in some cases improve response rates by up to 21 times. The role of the headline and each subsequent sentence is simply to get the reader to read the next sentence. Effective advertising is like a soap opera: each sentence should leave you wanting more, so you read the next sentence to see what happens! Unfortunately, the content of our consultant's original ad was less-than-inspiring consultant jargon that most business people would not relate to, so it is unlikely that anyone even read the whole ad."

"So, while the headline and subhead helped, they couldn't completely counteract the lame content of the ad itself?"

"That's it exactly. StreetSmart Marketers know that to write effective advertising, you not only need a great headline; you also need to understand the underlying needs, fears, desires and wants of your target market, and include the information in your copy. If you do that, you will grab their attention and draw them through your advertising until they reach your call to action."

"I guess," Lindsay pondered, "you can apply those advertising concepts to any form of advertising or promotion, including direct mail marketing efforts..."

"Absolutely," the StreetSmart Marketer confirmed. "It almost doesn't matter what business you're in, direct mail properly executed works. Sometimes it may not be economical if you sell a low-priced item, but a well crafted letter can get a prospect to take action. Direct mail specialists always say that direct mail is simply salesmanship in print, yet many direct response letters written by untrained people fail to sell and to follow six basic rules."

"Six basic rules? Lindsay asked.

"Yes," the StreetSmart Marketer smiled, removing a slip of paper from his jacket pocket. "I was going to include this with your Key 7 discussion summary at the end of our talk, but I think you may as well have it now to give it a read-over."

With that, he handed her a single page list titled: '6 Simple Rules for Creating Direct Mail That Gets Your Phone to Ring':

1. You must have a headline that attracts attention. The headline is the most important part of a direct response letter and changing it can result in 200-300% gains in response, even when nothing else is changed.

2. If you don't create instant interest and value, people won't read even the shortest letter. Creating interest and value can get the longest letters read more than once.

3. Social proof is one of the most powerful tools available to the direct response marketer. Use lots of testimonials showing that you can deliver what you claim. People want to know that you can deliver what you claim. Other proof mechanisms include specific details, numbers. The more specific you are, the more your claims will be believed.

4. Write to people in a personal manner. Write to them in the same way you speak to people. Worry more about clearly communicating your message than the quality of your English prose. Use slang, use contractions and remember in copywriting it's OK to begin a sentence with "And."

5. Demonstrate that what you are offering is a bargain. Unless your prospect feels that what you are offering has value and that she is getting more in results than you are asking in costs, she won't take action. Make your offer as free of risk as possible.

6. Show people how easy it is to order, by explaining exactly what to do and making ordering easy. The more complex you make it the fewer orders you will receive! So keep it simple, interesting, informative and effective.

"I'll frame this," Lindsay smiled, "after I give copies to staff."

"I'm very happy to be of service," The StreetSmart Marketer winked, as he took another sip of coffee. "I'd now like to discuss the role of the small business CEO as an allocator of resources."

"Fire when ready – I'm all ears," Lindsay enthused.

"Alright, the first thing I should mention is that the primary job of a business owner is to continually look for ways to increase the rate of return on the equity in their business. This is true if you are a sole practitioner or the head of a large multi-national. As owners of small businesses we don't always realize this. Many of us think our primary job is to bring in new business, and in some cases your earning ability is your only equity. But even when our only equity is our earning ability, we still have to decide how to allocate our resources. On whom do we spend our time? On which products do we focus? Which of our skills do we use most?"

"Interesting," Lindsay observed, "I'd never really considered attaching measurable criteria to how efficiently I spend my time. Yet, it's true that my main source of equity is my earning ability so I need to focus on good use of time, product promotion and skills."

"Indeed, in a recent article by renowned speaker, author and consultant Brian Tracy, he suggested this equity is your ability to think and act in ways that generate results. So to improve your return on your equity – that's everything you have invested in the business, not only money – you have to invest your resources in those areas with higher potential returns."

"Not that I actually *have* a lot of resources," Lindsay winced.

"Resources are scarce in every business, Lindsay. None of us has enough time, money or good people to do everything we need to do. What this means to owners of small businesses is that you have to be constantly finding ways to maximize your returns on every activity, so that you increase your earning ability or at least produce the same result with less effort."

"I think I do need to be a bit more diligent in maximizing returns *and* reducing effort," Lindsay realized.

"That's an important recognition to arrive at. Street-Smart Marketers make sure that every activity they undertake is the highest and best use of their time. They know time spent on any activity that does not yield maximum results is gone forever. They continually find ways of producing better results from the same or fewer resources. As a business owner you owe it to yourself to ensure that every marketing activity yields the maximum output. As you've heard me say before, it costs the same to run a marketing program that yields one or two sales as it does to run one that produces constant sales."

Lindsay nodded agreement. "I find it often helps me to fully understand concepts if there's a practical example I can relate to. Do you have such an example you can share?"

"I do. I was talking recently to Allan, a contact management software consultant, about his marketing activities. He said he had tried a number of marketing activities, including direct mail, which yielded poor to modest results and he did not believe that anything but referrals worked in his business. He said he realized he needed better marketing but was frustrated by results and needed help."

The StreetSmart Marketer took another drink of coffee and continued. "After discussing Allan's advertising and direct mail activities, it became clear that his poor results were not that these strategies don't work in his business. It was more a function of his lack of knowledge, than their ineffectiveness. The question for him was; 'As an allocator of resources, should he be focussing on what works, i.e. referrals, or should he learn how to do other forms of marketing that generate greater results from the meagre resources available?' I believe the answer identifies both. Do more of what works, and learn additional ways to bring in new prospects."

"And did he take both of these steps?" Lindsay asked.

"Yes. I showed him how he could create a greater response by improving the headline of his ads and letters. We also discussed making a more compelling offer that would encourage people to respond. He called me back a few weeks later to excitedly tell me that the changes we'd made had resulted in a 45 per cent increase in response rates and a 38 per cent increase in new business. No additional cost; no additional effort. He is not finished yet. He is now working on ways to increase both the response rate and the gross dollars he gets from each new customer."

"Good for him!" Lindsay enthused.

"This is a perfect example of the impact of leverage; you take what's working modestly, or even poorly, and make it better. You never accept any level of response as the ceiling. Anything less than that and you are failing your stakeholders: i.e. yourself, your family and your customers. Why? Because you have to work that much harder than you need to, to produce the results you are producing. This increases your costs, reduces your free time, reduces your return on the time you do invest and limits the time available for creative thinking about your business."

"I'm seeing that we can probably keep our recent advertising and direct mail budgets intact and simply do both activities in a smarter, more effective way without adding to costs," Lindsay concluded.

"That sounds like a very astute approach to take, Lindsay. Business owners often tell me 'Direct Mail doesn't work in my business!' or 'Advertising doesn't work in my business!' They don't realize that these tools take skill and experience, and that these skills can be relatively easily learned. Just because you can write a letter, does not mean you understand the rules of successful direct mail. Once they understand leverage, they don't accept low results any longer; they begin to learn, to re-think and to find ways to improve the results. They also are no longer prepared to accept the default of referrals and networking. There is no question that both these other techniques work, but at some point they become a limiting factor in your growth if they're all you ever use."

Lindsay nodded agreement. "When I first met you, apart from a little advertising, we largely confined ourselves to referrals and networking, not realizing how limiting this really was. I now think firms that restrict themselves in this manner really need to ask themselves: If they feel that referrals and networking are the only marketing tools that really work in their business, what impact is that having on their ability to grow or to have more time off?"

"Well put, Lindsay. I'd now like to discuss the power of a single action website, which immediately raises the question: Does your website produce what you expect from it? In my experience most websites, including one of mine, achieve very little, despite my having spent considerable sums of money on search engine optimization, key words and so on. Good page ranking by Google seems to have questionable benefit. When you get a lot of traffic as a result of web-based promotions, you often get a lot of very unqualified traffic, so often conversion rates are very low."

"So what can anyone do to change this?"

"Well, it seems that the prevailing wisdom says it is important to give prospects lots of choice. Prevailing wisdom also suggests letting the customer control the sales process. Another popular belief is that people don't read on the web, so you have to be very brief. I quickly grew tired of my poor results. I am impatient and I also don't like to keep repeating things that don't produce results. Quite frankly the conventional wisdom didn't seem to be working for me. So I sought the advice of Bob Serling, an information products marketer who writes an e-zine called Direct Marketing Insider. Based on what I have learned from Bob and my own experience, I now believe that this prevailing wisdom is preventing many sites from achieving their full potential."

"Can you elaborate on that?" Lindsay asked.

"Sure, Bob has pioneered the Single Action Websites (SAW) concept. SAW's do exactly what they say. On a SAW you can only do one thing. This means you have to have a very clear strategy and that you have to market your products or services one at a time. This could be a challenge if you have a large number of products; however for my purposes it made sense."

"How so?"

"On my Results Exchange site, there are dozens of choices of things you can attend, look at, read, see, listen to and so on. Rather than re-work this site, I created a brand new website packed with useful information. I also wanted to be able to assess them side by side. The new site is designed only to get visitors to sign up for this newsletter. If you would like to see a SAW in action please take a look at www.streetsmartmarketer.com I think you will find it instructional. Taking a leaf out of direct response marketing, Bob Serling believes that all the choice you get on a "cafeteria" site confuses prospects and most end-up doing nothing."

"I think that's very true," Lindsay agreed.

"But when you go to the streetsmartmarketer.com website there's a promo letter for my newsletter, an archive of past issues and a subscription form for new subscribers. You can't buy anything; you can't see pictures of me playing golf or of my kids and you can't download anything other than past issues. Although the site is new and I have not had time to drive traffic to the site, our conversion rate for visitors to the site has increased from less than 5 per cent of visitors opting-in to about 60 per cent opting-in. I would call that a success. Also we are getting more new subscribers from the new site than from the old even though we have not promoted it."

The StreetSmart Marketer finished his coffee and tossed the empty cardboard cup in a waste bin. "I'd like to spend the last bit of our meeting going over a few overall strategies to boost your advertising results"

"Sounds good," Lindsay smiled.

"Here are a few things to pay attention to. As mentioned when we talked about direct marketing, you need to get your prospect's undivided attention and the way to do this is with a strong headline that speaks to their dreams, desires, fears and frustrations. Your headline offers the reader a bribe, in the form of a strong benefit, in return for reading the ad. Encourage readers to read your whole message by showing them how you'll bring value to their lives. Offer immediate proof of your claim, and testimonials are one of the most valuable but undervalued ways of convincing prospects you can meet their needs. Everyone wants a bargain. You must convince your prospects that what they spend with you is minimal compared to the benefits they'll receive. And finally, make it easy to buy from you. Everyone is secretly asking to be lead, so tell your prospects exactly what action to take to buy from you and show them how easy it is to order."

"My thanks as always for your advice," Lindsay beamed. "Shall we meet here again this time next week?"

"I don't see why not," the StreetSmart Marketer concurred as he held his hand out to feel drops of moisture. "I think it's starting to rain… and since neither of us has an umbrella…"

"I hear you," Lindsay laughed as she quickly rose from the bench. "We'd best both make a mad dash if we want to get back to our offices without getting drenched…"

KEY 7:
Creating effective advertising:

1. Marketing for small business isn't a beauty contest. You should really run only direct response, not image advertising. Direct response is 100 per cent measurable and if done properly, you get the image advertising free.

2. Simply changing a headline has been shown to double or triple response rates and in some cases improve response rates by up to 21 times.

3. Effective advertising is like a soap opera: each sentence should leave you wanting more, so you read the next sentence to see what happens.

4. You not only need a great headline; you need to know the underlying needs, fears, desires and wants of your target market, and include the information in your copy. Apart from the headline, the offer is the next most important element in your advertising.

5. If you don't create instant interest and value, people won't read even the shortest letter. Creating interest and value can get the longest letters read more than once.

6. Social proof is one of the most powerful tools available to the direct response marketer. Use lots of testimonials showing that you can deliver what you claim. People want to know that you can deliver what you claim. Other proof mechanisms include specific details, numbers. The more specific you are, the more your claims will be believed.

7. Write to people in a personal manner. Write to them in the same way you speak to people. Worry more about clearly communicating your message than the quality of your English prose. Use slang, use contractions and remember in copywriting it's OK to begin a sentence with "And."

8. Continually find ways of producing better results from the same or fewer resources. As a business owner you owe it to yourself to ensure that every marketing activity yields the maximum output.

9. Everyone is secretly asking to be lead, so tell your prospects exactly what action to take to buy from you and show them how easy it is to order.

8

"What you can do, or dream you can do, begin it! Boldness has genius, power and magic in it."
- **Wolfgang von Goethe**

KEY 8:
Expanding Buying Behaviour:

Once a customer has bought from you, expand buying behavior as they're predisposed to buy again. Expanding buying behavior means up-selling or cross-selling at the point of sale, it means programming sales in advance and it means offering other products and services as a back end stream of revenue to maximize the customer relationship.

A late summer breeze blew Lindsay's hair back as she crossed the street carrying two cardboard cups of coffee. As she entered the park, she saw the StreetSmart Marketer arriving at their familiar shared bench, a newspaper tucked under his arm.

On reaching him, she quickly handed him a coffee and plopped down on the bench beside him.

"Hello Lindsay," he greeted her, "How's everything in the world of business these days?"

"Just wonderful, thanks," Lindsay beamed. "It seems the more we follow your advice, the better we do."

"That's a tough one to figure out, isn't it?" the StreetSmart Marketer quipped dryly. "It seems we're on to something good."

"We sure are you big tease – thanks to your advice of course."

"No room for improvement then?"

"Well, we could always use more customers…"

"More customers? Or might you achieve greater levels of success if you just got the existing customers to buy more?"

"Well, that would work too of course – but how do you go about making that happen?"

"I'll take that as my cue to start today's discussion on Key 8: Expanding Buying Behaviour. I have to leave a little early today as I'm meeting up with clients. So, I'll start right in now: The first item to explore is the need to grow your profits by encouraging your existing customers to increase their spending each time they buy. Once a customer has bought from you, expand buying behavior as they're predisposed to buy again. Expanding buying behavior means up-selling or cross-selling at the point of sale, it means programming sales in advance and it means offering other products and services as a back end stream of revenue to maximize the customer relationship. I always maintain that the quickest way to grow your business is not by adding new customers, but by encouraging existing customers to buy more or buy more often."

"Can you explain how this can be done – and give me an example? Lindsay asked.

"Sure, one way to get customers to buy more is by removing the lowest-priced options made available to them, especially if these items are just as costly for you to provide as the higher-priced item, or nearly so. Simply put, if you want to increase profits, trim low-profit-margin items from your product line. They may be eating up limited and valuable resources that could be better utilized elsewhere. And here's an example of such innovative StreetSmart thinking by one of North America's great entrepreneurs: Tom Monaghan, the founder of Domino's Pizza, related a story to *Fortune Small Business* magazine in which he recalled an incident in the early days in his first pizzeria: He said that one night, most of his employees didn't turn up for work."

"Wow – the poor guy was in a real jam," Lindsay observed.

"He sure was – though I don't think he'd qualify as a *poor guy* – and he was unsure whether or not he should even open the pizzeria. Someone suggested that since there wasn't much manpower on hand, they should just eliminate the six-inch personal pizzas – the smallest and least-pricey pizza of the five sizes they made – to simplify operations. Monaghan noted that the six-inch pizza cost almost as much to make and took just as long to make as the larger pizzas – and it took just as much time to deliver it. But since the price was much lower, it brought in far less money. Monaghan decided to give this a try."

"So what happened?" Lindsay asked.

"Many customers who would have order the little pizza simply moved up to the next size when told the smallest one was not available. Monaghan recalls that the shop never got busy that night 'yet we made 50 per cent more money than we ever had.' The next night they eliminated the nine-inch pizza size and were able to get caught up on all the bills. By reducing the options to medium, large and extra-large, the pizzeria was making far more profit on every delivery. Monaghan says he learned then that 'keeping things simple could be more profitable.' And he's right."

"That's amazing." Lindsay exclaimed, "but when you think about it, it makes a great deal of sense – not only where the time and production, delivery and driver costs the same, but staff would have had to have been trained to make the smaller size and those little pizzas might have taken up baking time that could have gone instead to the larger more profitable pizzas."

"It's true, it all adds up pretty quickly," the StreetSmart Marketer agreed. "Lindsay, sometimes discoveries like this are forced upon us; sometimes we are smart enough to figure it out. Whichever way it happens, as business owners, we must always look for ways to increase the dollar amount at the point of purchase, or offer existing customers a reason to come back more often. If you could get each and every one of your customers to spend just 10 per cent more each time they buy from you, what impact would that have on your bottom line? Go ahead do the calculations; I am sure you will be shocked."

"I've just done some very rough calculations in my head, and you're right, I am shocked – that's a lot of extra revenue and profit with no added investment on our part."

"Well, I hate to dash, but as I mentioned, I have to leave early today – so, I trust you gained some useful, helpful information and insight today?" the StreetSmart Marketer wondered as he handed Lindsay a summary of the day's discussions.

"Amen to that – and thank you again for such terrific advice," Lindsay smiled. "Well, you mentioned you have to go and I guess I should be getting back to the office as well. We'll meet same time and place next week?"

"Actually," the StreetSmart Marketer said as he tossed his cardboard cup in a waste bin, "I'm going to need that time to prepare for a seminar that evening…"

"Oh," Lindsay said quietly, "alright, then..."

Noticing Lindsay's crestfallen look, he added: "But you're very welcome to attend and we'll be going over the content of the ninth key: the need to test everything. I've jotted the hotel name, location and room and the seminar start time on your summary sheet. It's a free seminar and we'll cover a lot of ground. I think you'll find it useful – will you be attending?"

"Of course," Lindsay said quickly, looking up from the summary sheet. "The hotel isn't far from here and I have that evening free... I'd love to attend."

"Great – I'll see you there."

With that, the two friends parted paths, each looking forward to the seminar ahead.

KEY 8:
Expanding Buying Behaviour

1. Once a customer has bought from you, expand buying behavior as they're predisposed to buy again. Expanding buying behavior means up-selling or cross-selling at the point of sale, it means programming sales in advance and it means offering other products and services as a back end stream of revenue to maximize the customer relationship.

2. The quickest way to grow your business is not by adding new customers, but by encouraging existing customers to buy more or buy more often.

3. To increase profits, trim low-profit-margin items from your product line. They may be eating up limited and valuable resources that could be better utilized elsewhere.

4. Business owners must always look for ways to increase the dollar amount at the point of purchase, or offer existing customers a reason to come back more often.

5. Getting each and every one of your customers to spend just 10 per cent more each time they buy from you, can have a tremendous impact on your bottom line.

9

"We can't be creative if we refuse to be confused. Change always starts with confusion; cherished interpretations must dissolve to make way for the new. When we're bold enough to move through the fear and enter the abyss, we rediscover we're creative"
-**Margaret Wheatley**

KEY 9:
Repeat Mailings and Free Reports:

If you only send a mailing out once you are only getting a fraction of what's possible in terms of response... Prospects need information to make buying decisions, and unless you give it to them they won't buy.

Lindsay pulled into the visitors' parking lot tucked behind the sprawling Toronto hotel. She checked her appearance in the car mirror, combed her hair and adjusted the straps on her dress. She was a little nervous as she walked towards the Hotel entrance, her high heels clacking on the concrete walkway.

Once inside, she followed a crowd of people filing into a meeting hall to hear StreetSmart Marketer Michael Hepworth give his speech and take part in the workshop and discussions that would follow.

Lindsay found an available seat near the back of the crowded room and sat down between an older woman and a much-older business executive with a handle bar moustache and goatee.

At the front of the room, holding onto a microphone, the StreetSmart Marketer was addressing the audience. "Greetings everyone – it's wonderful to see so many of you come out on a sultry summer evening. I know some of you – perhaps most of you – will want to get back home later this evening to sit out and enjoy the lovely weather – so I'll get right to it and open with a question: How often should you repeat a mailing? ...Anyone?

A quick sip of water and he continued. "I'm not surprised not one of you had a ready answer for that question – it's not an easy question to answer. I am often asked this question and usually my answer is that you should repeat a mailing at least two or three times if it works the first time. I will explain why in a moment. First though, here are some specific results that I think illustrate the impact of multiple impressions of the same advertisement to a single list: Dick Larkin, The Yellow Pages Commando – and if you haven't subscribed to his newsletter, you're missing a gem – and I once did a teleseminar together. We both sent invitations to our respective readers. We received a total of 226 registrations. The first invitation went out two weeks before the teleseminar. From this first round we received 31 registrations, which turned out to be only 13 per cent of the registrations. We waited a week and then did a daily invitation for four days. The last invitation being sent on the day of the teleseminar."

The elderly gentleman sitting next to Lindsay put up his hand: "Can you share with us all of the percentages from each mailing?"

"Of course. Here's what happened: The second invitation created 23 per cent of the registrations, the third created 43.8 per cent, the fourth brought in 12.3 per cent and the fifth brought in 5.3 per cent. Any questions?"

Lindsay put up her hand. "So what do we learn from this?"

"That's a good question, Lindsay. I guess the first thing we've learned is that if you only send a mailing out once you are only getting a fraction of what's possible in terms of response. We can also see that repeated mailings generate a classic bell curve of responses; and that mailings that arrive fast and furiously don't negatively affect customer relationships and in fact increase your business. So, if you do direct mail, e-mail marketing or any other kind of direct response, don't sell yourself short by only sending out one round of advertising. You should also test everything – never assume you know what your market wants; always test and keep only items that add revenue and/or profit."

The discussion continued, followed by a brief break before The StreetSmart Marketer returned to conclude the program with a more informal session.

"Folks; we're back," he began. "As a bit of a change of pace, I'd like to share with all of you what I learned from a granddad doing magic tricks."

A quick sip of water and he continued. "While waiting at San Diego's airport for a plane back home, I had watched a granddad entertain his grandson with a few simple magic tricks. Now, I have always been fascinated by magic. I know it's not really magic and I always try to figure out how such tricks are done. Sometimes I am pretty sure I know the answers, but it still fascinates me. Watching the two having fun together, got me thinking; magic and marketing are in some ways very similar."

"How?" someone in the audience asked.

"Well, you think you know how something is done, but unless you know the secret and practice a little, you are not going to get the result you are looking for. And even the simplest marketing technique requires you to know exactly how to execute it and also requires a certain amount of practice. When making suggestions for marketing programs, I often hear 'I tried that and it didn't work!' This is especially true in discussions with owners of services business, particularly professional services. I frequently hear that nothing works to grow their businesses except for referrals and networking. While I can't deny the experiences of these people, the truth is that every business can benefit from some kind of direct outreach program like advertising and direct mail."

"Direct mail doesn't work for me," a businessman in the front row grumbled.

"Ah, I don't know if everyone heard that, but someone has just said direct mail doesn't work for them. However, could it be that if it doesn't work for you, you are not doing it right? Could it be that you don't know the 'secret'? After all, it is one thing to know about a technique, it is quite another to be able to execute it well. The real problem with many of the people who have tried a particular strategy and found it produced no results, is that they have assumed they know what to do. They think they've followed the basic rules, and understood all the elements that have to be effectively executed to ensure success. Mostly this is not true."

"Can you give us an example?" the woman seated next to Lindsay asked. "It would help make this a bit clearer in my mind."

"Alright, for example, Ed has a successful business that sells supports and pillows for people with back and neck pain. Among other things he's been advertising in one of those free booklets, full of advertisements, which get left in your mailbox. The results have been very poor. With each issue, he had had only three to five responses – and no sales. The lack of results is frustrating: It costs him money every time he runs the ad, but if he is to grow he knows he can't give up. Was the ad wrong, was the publication wrong, or was the offer wrong? He just didn't know…"

"So what was wrong?" a young woman in a pin-striped suit asked from the middle of the audience. "What was the problem?"

"That's a good question: What was wrong? Ed had a great product, great service and good sums of money spent regularly on advertising. And yet, sales were few and far between. After reviewing the ad, it became clear that even if it had been seen by his target audience, it would not have yielded the results he needed. There was no attention getting headline; just his company name and logo…"

"That's it?" someone asked.

"Yes, that's it. Many of us make the same mistake. Unless you're a household name, no one knows who you are – and what's more no one cares. Your company name and logo are possibly the least important elements of your advertisement. What is needed is a strong headline that creates interest and encourages the reader to read on. It has been proven over and over again; the headline is the most important element of an advertisement. Simply changing it and nothing else in an ad can improve response by 200 or 300 per cent. But there were other things wrong with the ad. There were too many items for sale in a limited space. There's a marketing axiom: 'If you try to sell everything, you sell nothing. If you try to sell everyone you sell nobody.' His ad was trying to do just that."

Another sip of water, and the StreetSmart Marketer continued. "There is another rule worth keeping mind. Never try to sell something in a medium where you can't afford to tell the whole story. Prospects need information to make buying decisions, and unless you give it to them they won't buy. Clearly, Ed had to change the strategy. He didn't want to spend more money on advertising until he knew it worked. He also couldn't buy a list of back pain sufferers. Chiropractors and doctors don't share such information. So he changed the strategy to one of finding back pain sufferers he could then market to. He decided to offer them one thing he could easily promote in the available space; a free report on how to control and prevent back and neck pain. The report would help them understand their back pain and what they could do about it. It would educate them on how his products could help, and position him as the leading logical choice."

"Good move," someone in the front muttered.

"I hope everyone heard that. Someone just commented that this change in strategy was a good move – and it certainly was. The ad was recreated with a strong headline: *How to Avoid, Control or Eliminate Back and Neck Pain Forever.* The ad offered a free report they could get simply by phoning a 1-800 number. So the space cost was the same, but there was now a compelling headline to draw people in. There was an offer of something that his target clients would want; the message was clear and simple. More importantly there were clear instructions on what to do."

"What were the results?" Lindsay asked.

"The results surprised even me. Ed's previous ads had generated no more than five inquiries. Within days of the new ad appearing, it produced more than 190 inquires. That is an improvement of more than 3,000 per cent! This is leverage in action; getting a much larger result with the same effort and money. He got leverage, by changing his strategy and learning how to execute each tactic effectively. Now that he knows it works, it becomes an easy task of finding other suitable places to advertise, and placing the ad. If placed in the publications his target audience read, the sales should come flooding in. Had you spoken to this business owner just a month ago, you would have found him doubtful of the value of advertising in his business. If you feel that a marketing technique you tried in your business produced disappointing results, could it be that you fell into the same kind of traps Ed did?"

Murmurs of agreement rippled through the audience. "The key," he continued, "is in knowing what to do, learning how to do it and actually doing it. Unfortunately most business owners assume they understand what to do and so when they try to execute, they fall flat on their faces and waste time and money. So, before you execute your next marketing activity, invest the time to learn how to do it right – or hire an expert. That way you will generate a much better result. Marketing that pays for itself is no longer a cost, it is an investment, but executing a marketing program without knowledge of the rules and skills to execute them effectively, is gambling. Marketing isn't magic but it takes insight and practice. Thank you all for coming – and I'll stay a bit longer if anyone wishes to speak with me individually."

Lindsay quickly made her way to the front to express her thanks. After chatting briefly, they agreed to meet again at the park.

KEY 9:
Repeat Mailings and Free Reports:

1. If you only send a mailing out once you are only getting a fraction of what's possible in terms of response..

2. Figure out what makes your business different or unique. Then, differentiate yourself from competitors. Advertising and marketing that's the same as everyone else's does as much for your competitors as it does for you. Marketing making the same claims as everyone else, forces customers to focus on one thing they do understand; price. This leads to an eroding of margins and a lack of customer loyalty.

3. Mailings that arrive fast and furiously don't negatively affect customer relationships and in fact increase your business.

4. The real problem with many of the people who have tried a particular strategy and found it produced no results, is that they wrongly assumed they knew what to do.

5. If you try to sell everything, you sell nothing. If you try to sell everyone you sell nobody.

6. Never try to sell something in a medium where you can't afford to tell the whole story. Prospects need information to make buying decisions, and unless you give it to them they won't buy.

7. Without paying anything more, you can get great results from a revamped ad with a compelling headline to draw people in and clear instruction on placing orders.

8. Before you execute your next marketing activity, invest the time to learn how to do it right – or hire an expert. That way you will generate a much better result.

10

"Being busy does not always mean real work. The object of all work is production or accomplishment and to either of these ends there must be forethought, system, planning, intelligence, and honest purpose, as well as perspiration. Seeming to do is not doing. Genius is one per cent inspiration and 99 per cent perspiration."
 -Thomas Alva Edison

"Time is our most valuable asset, yet we tend to waste it, kill it, and spend it, rather than invest it."
 - Jim Rohn

"If management makes bad decisions in order to hit short-term earnings targets and consequently gets behind the eight-ball in terms of costs, customer satisfaction or brand strength, no amount of subsequent brilliance will overcome the damage that has been inflicted."
 - Warren Buffett

KEY 10:
Strategic Time Allocation:

Strategic Time Allocation: Make time for creativity and for working on the business, as well as in it. Time off is also critical.

Gentle summer breezes caressed Lindsay's face as she made her way through the park, coffees in hand. The StreetSmart Marketer was just up ahead, seated on the bench, quietly reading his newspaper.

"Your coffee, sir," Lindsay greeted him. The StreetSmart Marketer set his paper down and accepted his coffee, immediately taking a long sip. "Oh that's very good," he smiled. "No matter how busy the day gets, you can always make time for a coffee."

"That's true for me too," Lindsay sighed, "though just barely – I seem to be working 24/7 most days just trying to keep up with the business, keep everything going... and there still isn't enough time to do the important things I want to do to achieve growth..."

"Sounds like you may have time-management problems," the StreetSmart Marketer considered. "It's a good thing today's topic is on the tenth key: Strategic Time Allocation; making time for creativity and for working on the business, as well as in it – and of course, time off is also critical."

"Of course, time off," Lindsay repeated. "But what *is* time off? I work most weekends and I haven't had a vacation in ages. I'd like to take time off, but I'm always too busy. And every time I tackle something important, I get sidetracked with other things..."

"Let me share with you one of the 6 Dirty Little Secrets about Building a Business Success. Your problems are addressed in all six secrets. But let's start with Dirty Little Secret number 1 – You Need Resolve to Keep You on Course. Many of us, who own our own businesses, are chiefly ideas people. Every day we have new ideas we want to execute. And everyday there are business opportunities that often appear more interesting than the one we are currently chasing down. But the problem is, if you don't focus, you will never grow. I don't agree with a lot of the popular presenters who talk about the need for multiple streams of income. Its not that I don't think this is a good strategy. It is, but only once you have one thing running well without a need for your constant input, should you move onto something else and begin to build it."

He paused a moment and then continued: "Most of these presenters are selling ways to generate additional streams of income, so don't you think there might be some bias in their advice? If you focus on too many things, you achieve little. One of my business partners always said; "If you chase two rabbits they both get away. You have to decide what really matters to you. You have to do some soul searching and you have to be honest with yourself. Once you know what you want, focus all of your attention on achieving it, and stay with it."

The StreetSmart Marketer took a sip of coffee and continued. "Something else that directly applies to you right now is Dirty Little Secret number 2: You don't just *find* time for important things – you have to *make* time. If you look at your resolutions and goals I think you will find that many of them never became reality simply because you didn't set aside the time to work on them."

"That's very true," Lindsay admitted.

"And it's also a common problem," the StreetSmart Marketer continued. "Many business owners spend so much time working in the business; they have no time for working on the business. You have to break the cycle by scheduling time every week in your calendar to work on important things. If they are important, make an appointment with yourself and treat these important matters like any other important appointment."

"I'll definitely make a point of doing that," Lindsay agreed. "Unfortunately, right now I spend so much time checking to make sure the sales people and others have done their jobs, making sure their work is on track and on time, checking the accuracy of what they're doing and making sure their doing everything they're supposed to be doing…"

"Wait a minute," the StreetSmart Marketer interjected, "aren't sales people supposed to be self-starters, professionals who know what they're doing, people who are capable of keeping schedules and meeting expectations? They're doing a good job aren't they?"

"Well sure," Lindsay concurred, "but it doesn't hurt to look over their shoulders and make sure they're doing all job aspects."

"Actually, it likely does hurt – it hurts you. It really sounds like you're doing a lot of unnecessary micro-managing of people who are better left alone to do their jobs. And the time you spend on such minor details is time you don't have to spend on major areas of importance. Dirty Little Secret number 3 – Many of Us Major in Minor Things – clearly applies here: When you own and run a business, you have to stop operating like a worker and begin to act like a boss. For most workers, work shows up and they do it. As a business owner, you have to decide what's most important, and work on that. You can't afford to get sidetracked by what's easy, or fun or less stressful. You have to decide what is most important and do it, or get it done. Your mantra has to be; "If it is to be, it's up to me."

"But what if everything doesn't get done?"

"Don't sweat the small stuff if it isn't done; it isn't the end of the world; particularly if you've got all the important stuff done."

"What if I don't have all the resources I need?"

"That question is answered quite nicely by Dirty Little Secret number 4 – Resourcefulness is More Important than Resources. Resources are important. You can't make any change happen until you know what resources you need to make it happen. You may need more resources or you may need different ones, but you need to define your requirements. Most small businesses are strapped for resources, be it money, people or equipment. But this should not stop you. You can get almost anything you want if you are resourceful. Somebody always has what you need, so once you find them there are many ways to get what you need. Try barter and joint ventures for starters."

"It sounds like a lot of this is quite doable if you're well organized." Lindsay observed.

"It is – and that brings us to Dirty Little Secret number 5 – Define the Next Step: Do you make lists of all the things you have to do, and then cross off each item as you do it? If so, you probably find your list never gets any shorter, and there are some tasks that never get done. One way around this, is to list every task you have, and at the same time define the outcome you desire and the next action you need to take to move this closer to reality. One of the reasons we don't take action, is that when we are busy we don't take the time to figure out the next step. Often the task looks like a big complex activity and we shy away from it, and start looking for something easier and quicker to do. Defining the next action step, helps break it down into smaller more achievable tasks and gets you moving forward. Every time you list a task – or delegate it to someone else – ask yourself; 'What's the next action here?' Write it down so you don't have to think of it next time you are looking at your list of to-do's."

"This is all terrific advice," Lindsay said enthusiastically.

"And this brings us to the final secret: Dirty Little Secret number 6 – Manage Your Time Strategically. As a business owner you have choices over how you spend your time. There is 'preparation time' that is for delegating tasks, planning your strategies and tactics. It's time for outlining your ideas and even for cleaning up stuff that's gone wrong. This is also the time you set aside for learning important new skills that will take you where you want to go. I personally make a point of studying new materials and ideas everyday. One of my biggest budget items is training. Then there's 'achievement time' that's for doing the things that make you money and move you toward your goals.

Finally there's 'rejuvenation time' and this is exactly what it sounds like; time off away from business recharging the batteries. This is where you do the things you love to do that have nothing to do with work."

"How do you actually go about managing your time strategically," Lindsay wondered aloud.

"You have to schedule this time and plan it. If you don't, it won't happen and you'll find your progress slowed. I personally only have 3 days per week where I am focused on 'achievement time' while I have one to two days of 'preparation time' and in the summer I try to have 2.5 days of 'rejuvenation Time'. I find working this way keeps me fresh and creative. At the same time, I get far more done. And most of what I get done is important stuff. If you work with these dirty little secrets you will find the changes imperceptible at first, but as they gather momentum and the work you put in begins to show the cumulative effects, you will be astonished at what happens in your business. We've now covered all six dirty little secrets to keep you on course and achieving what you set out to achieve when you started out."

"Thank you so much – I know all of this will really make a difference," Lindsay smiled.

"You're very welcome, Lindsay, and please understand that everything you do in business makes a difference and has an impact; good or bad. Here's an inspiring quote from investment expert Warren Buffett: 'Every day, in countless ways, the competitive position of each of our businesses grows either weaker or stronger. If we are delighting customers, eliminating unnecessary costs, and improving products and services, we gain strength. But if we treat customers with indifference or tolerate bloat, our businesses will wither. On a daily basis, the effects of our actions are imperceptible; cumulatively, though, their consequences are enormous. When our long-term competitive position improves as a result of these almost unnoticeable actions, we describe the phenomenon as widening the moat. And doing that is essential if we are to have the kind of business we want a decade or two from now. We always, of course, hope to earn more money in the short-term. But when short-term and long-term conflict, widening the moat must take precedence. If management makes bad decisions in order to hit short-term earnings targets and consequently gets behind the eight ball in terms of costs, customer satisfaction or brand strength, no amount of subsequent brilliance will overcome the damage that has been inflicted."

"That Mr. Buffet is such a brilliant man."

"And his words should cause us to examine the way we do business and ask ourselves questions such as: Are you continuously finding ways to delight customers, eliminate unnecessary costs, and improve your products and services? If so, your business is probably gaining strength. If not, you are not standing still, you are definitely going backwards. After all, to win in business takes continuous hard work. There are almost no businesses left that don't require hard work if you want them to grow beyond providing you with a reasonable living and having something to do everyday. Believe me; I have looked for a long time. I have not found one and if you know of one please let me know. Every day I speak to people who want to grow their business but I find very few who are willing to develop the skills and focus it takes to be successful. So, most of them remain small, scratching out a living but with no real prospects for rapid growth or true prosperity."

"I *definitely* want *much* more than that for our printing business," Lindsay emphasized. "But even if I can completely eliminate micromanaging as you've suggested and I organize my time better, I know I'll still have more work than I can handle..."

"I certainly hear you," the StreetSmart Marketer interjected sympathetically. "Most business owners, especially those with rapidly growing businesses have far too many tasks on their plates. How do they juggle all the priorities? It seems that the only way is to either delegate or to simply drop some of the tasks. I know of a few ways you can go about dropping tasks and get more leverage on your time – and if you'd like I'll share them with you now."

"Please do."

"Each day, take a look at each of your scheduled tasks and decide if your business will suffer if you don't do it. If the answer is no, just don't do it. You can also lower your standards..."

"You must be joking," Lindsay said incredulously.

"Let me finish: You can lower your standards regarding certain relatively unimportant tasks. For example, you may pride yourself on personally replying to every email – but do you really need to respond to all of them, or is it enough to simply read the important ones. Many are sent simply to keep you informed."

"And a lot of emails, even from customers, are mass emails that really don't apply to me and I get a lot of junk email, spam and so on," Lindsay noted. "It does take time to go through it and read – so I think I'll delete more of the junk and only reply to the important emails where my input is being sought. That should save a lot of time."

"You can also force yourself to reduce your workload by guarding your time. This is all about setting some reasonable expectations for yourself. For example, instead of working every weekend, guard your weekends jealously. Spend the time with family or doing things you love. If you do this, you will find you are unable to complete all the work that you did before. This will force you to drop, delegate or redefine completion."

Lindsay nodded. "I'm beginning to realize that effective strategic management of my time is possible – but it can also be a fairly difficult thing to achieve, especially with so many variables and unknowns in the course of a business week."

"That's very true. Putting a plan in place will help; putting a strategy in place will help. But from time to time a crisis or problem will arise that you'll have to deal with by stepping outside the structure you've made. Fortunately, having a good strategy means such disruptions are rare and temporary, allowing you to return to your weekends off and delegating of responsibilities. It's also true that every now and then a problem comes along that stumps us and slows us down. Ask yourself, have you ever had a business problem that stopped you dead? One minute you're going along fine, the next minute you're stuck, not sure how to move forward."

"I sure have," Lindsay confirmed.

"I'd like to share with you some observations from a meeting Rick Wolfe of Poststone Corporation and I had with a group of successful business owners to discuss how to problem-solve in situations where you are slowed considerably or stopped entirely. My view is was not that successful entrepreneurs have fewer problems or different problems; it's just that they cope better with problems and don't allow them to stop their forward momentum. I've learned that effective problem-solvers relentlessly look for the right or a better question to answer."

The StreetSmart Marketer took a sip of coffee, adding: "And effective problem-solvers take action early and decisively, mostly with little concern over making the wrong decision. This is in sharp contrast to some people who find that until they can see the whole situation, they tend to do nothing and this can mean a long time of inaction on something that needs immediate attention. But our business owners noted action can mean the difference between success and failure. The key is to begin an action. A prevailing view among our decisive business owners was that sometimes it is much better to make a wrong decision now, than to make the right decision later. The key is to get moving. This seems to fly in the face of conventional wisdom; collecting your facts first before making a decision. Perhaps this is one of the distinguishing features of successful business owners. When you can't see the full picture, a solution to get yourself moving is to ask: 'What is the smallest thing I can do to move this situation forward?' This question gets you moving, and movement creates results."

"While inertia gets you... nowhere," Lindsay surmised.

"Quite," the StreetSmart Marketer smiled. "Another key trait was that these business builders tend to follow their gut instincts. While many problem solvers like to get input from peers and specialists, at the end of the day, they know it is up to them, and gut feel decides a lot of tough alternatives. One way to listen to your gut, even if you think you don't know the answer, is to do the traditional coin flip and tell yourself; "Heads I do, Tails I don't." Notice your immediate reaction when you see the result. If your reaction is disappointment, you know the other route is favoured by your gut. Go with what you favour; you are less likely to be wrong. Many of the participants found it helps to write down alternatives you may want to consider. Asses the risk. Ask what the difference between doing and not doing is. Often you will find the negative consequences of not taking action, greater than the negative consequence of taking the wrong action. Following these suggestions may improve your problem-solving ability, but note that your best ideas don't come unless there is challenge. That may mean you won't get the right answer the first time. But if you keep going at it, you probably will – and you will have learned a whole lot along the way."

"I certainly am learning a lot," Lindsay smiled.

"And speaking of learning, realize that you can learn anything you want. Like most business owners, you're likely too busy to read sufficiently to learn everything you need to run your business. If you would like to read more than you do, but don't have the time, consider reading book summaries. Most books only contain one or two principle ideas. These and the key points can usually be captured and distilled into a short summary saving you the necessity of reading the whole book. Take a look at the summaries available at www.summary.com. You can stay up to date with the latest business literature; expand your knowledge quickly and save money at the same time."

The StreetSmart Marketer paused a moment to finish his coffee, then continued. "Part of problem-solving involves searching for better questions – because these can lead to better answers. To paraphrase a much longer Einstein quote; 'There is no secret in the universe that will not yield its answers to a better line of questioning.' The first practice is that of reframing the question. Asking a question just one way only yields one set of answers, but by reframing the question, all of a sudden new possibilities are seen. The best problem-solvers seem to do this continuously. And one way to do this is to ask yourself; 'What's the question behind the question? Other questions you can ask yourself are: What's the real question or what's the true question? If you can get to a question with a yes or no answer, then you have probably gotten to the essence of your question and your decision becomes easier."

"How can I do this in a methodical way," Lindsay pondered.

"A good way to go about this is to ask yourself the '5 whys' to help you understand your motives and desired outcomes. As an example, imagine you find sales in your business falling despite an increased focus and spending on marketing. You might ask yourself these questions: 1. Why is this happening? Answer: The market is becoming immune to traditional approaches. 2. Why is the market becoming immune to traditional approaches? Answer: Everyone in our industry is doing things in the same way and so in the customers' view we are all undifferentiated. 3. Why is everyone marketing the same way? Answer: Because there is no one to challenge the thinking and no fresh blood is being brought in? 4. Why is no fresh blood being brought in? Answer: We have not seen the need previously. 5. Why have we not seen the need? Answer: Business has been good and we've all been comfortable, fat and happy? This line of questioning brings you to a different level of understanding than your first question. If you keep going you will find further answers."

"I've already found an incredible number of answers and terrific approaches to doing business – thanks to you," Lindsay said warmly. "The time has really gone by quickly and I've learned so much. Is it really true our next meeting, next week, is our last meeting?"

"I'm afraid so. I'll be leaving on a lengthy vacation in Africa just a couple of days after our meeting… but perhaps you can brief me on how you're doing on my return in a month's time?"

"I'd like that," Lindsay replied. "I'll look for you in the park."

"I'll be there. Meanwhile, here's the Key 10 summary to read over – and I'll see you next week for our closing discussion."

KEY 10:
Strategic Time Allocation

1. Force yourself to reduce your workload by guarding your time. This is all about setting some reasonable expectations for yourself. For example, instead of working every weekend, guard your weekends jealously.

2. If you focus on too many things, you achieve little. If you chase two rabbits they both get away. You have to decide what really matters to you.

3. You don't just *find* time for important things – you have to *make* time.

4. As a business owner, you have to decide what's most important, and work on that. You can't afford to get sidetracked by what's easy, or fun or less stressful. You have to decide what is most important and do it, or get it done.

5. Most small businesses are strapped for resources, be it money, people or equipment. But this should not stop you. You can get almost anything you want if you are resourceful. Somebody always has what you need, so once you find them there are many ways to get what you need. Try barter and joint ventures for starters.

6. Part of problem-solving involves searching for better questions – because these can lead to better answers. Ask yourself why when examining a problem and with each answer ask who again, five times in total.

7. If you would like to read more than you do, but don't have the time, consider reading book summaries. Most books only contain one or two principle ideas. These and the key points can usually be captured and distilled into a short summary.

8. Manage Your Time Strategically. As a business owner you have choices over how you spend your time. For example, there is 'preparation time' that is for delegating tasks, planning your strategies and tactics.

9. Everything you do in business makes a difference and has an impact; good or bad.

10. Each day, take a look at each of your scheduled tasks and decide if your business will suffer if you don't do it. If the answer is no, just don't do it.

11. Effective problem-solvers take action early and decisively, mostly with little concern over making the wrong decision. This is in sharp contrast to some people who find that until they can see the whole situation, they tend to do nothing and this can mean a long time of inaction on something that needs immediate attention.

11

"Vision is the art of seeing the invisible"
- **Jonathon Swift**

"We'd all have 20/20 vision if we could use the benefit of hindsight"
- **Sergeant Max Roswell**, Rhodesian Army, Corps of Engineers

"If you don't get referrals, you haven't earned them."
- **Jim Cecil**

"Leverage is like Star Wars' 'The Force': It's what entrepreneurs do to become successful, it's all around us, but we don't recognize it as such. But if you understand it and learn its power, then you are able to make much more consistent, strategic and proactive use of it."
- **Rick Spence**, former editor of Profit Magazine

KEY 11:
Leverage and Mentoring:

Leverage is simply the ability to create a large return with a small amount of effort. You can get leverage on your own assets and you can get leverage on other peoples' assets. The leverage you obtain from mentors can provide a shortcut to great success.

There was a light mist in the air as Lindsay found the StreetSmart Marketer standing by the park bench, reading his newspaper. "Why don't you have a seat instead of standing there, ignoring our comfortable bench?" she asked on handing him his coffee.

"The bench is a bit moist from the mist – and I've been sitting so much lately, that I really feel the need to stretch my legs," he replied. "Are you up for a walk?"

"Sure – why not?" Lindsay answered. The two hiked along a different path, one taking them to the far side of duck pond to a clearing in the woods.

"That's enough of a leg-stretch for now," the StreetSmart Marketer commented, motioning for Lindsay to join him in sitting down on a large fallen tree. "Nature's finest sofa is ours today."

"This is nice," Lindsay concurred, "and the canopy from the trees is keeping everything dry."

"Just like I planned," the StreetSmart Marketer laughed. "I thought we might talk about the advantages of leverage today."

"Interesting," Lindsay considered. "I've heard that leverage can be an effective way of growing a business, but to be honest, I don't really know what leverage is."

"Leverage is widely misunderstood, but it can be the key that unlocks the door to growing your business. For example, one fellow I know developed a series of modular training programs to help people manage their lives better. They're excellent programs, but there is a problem. He only knew a relatively small number of suitable prospects. He solved this problem with leverage – by going through coaches and consultants working with people who would make good prospects for his training programs. This may appear as a simple solution, but in fact it is a perfect example of leverage. And leverage is what I believe makes all the difference in business. But what is leverage? Almost everyone uses the word, but how many of us truly understand it. At a simple level, it is simply the ability to create a large return with a small amount of effort. You can get leverage on your own assets and you can get leverage on other peoples' assets. In this fellow's case, he is leveraging other peoples' client bases. These people have spent hundreds of dollars, or even thousands of dollars building their client bases. They have also spent countless hours building their client bases. Through leverage, he's able to tap into this investment and take advantage of it, with only a relatively small investment of both time and cash."

The StreetSmart Marketer took a sip of his coffee and then continued. "Rick Spence, former editor of Profit Magazine and now a consultant to business owners, discussed leverage in an email he wrote to me. Rick said: 'Leverage is like Star Wars' 'The Force': It's what entrepreneurs do to become successful, it's all around us, but we don't recognize it as such. But if you understand it and learn its power, then you are able to make much more consistent, strategic and proactive use of it.' Rick is right, we don't recognize it, but it is what successful entrepreneurs do. Almost every time they do something, they find ways to turn a small amount of input into a large output. They find opportunities where most people don't think to look."

"So where do we begin to look for leverage opportunities?" Lindsay asked as she sipped her coffee.

"It's important to recognize that every asset we have is leverage-able. Time is being the scarcest and most important asset for entrepreneurs to master. But what else can we leverage? How about under-utilized assets like intellectual property? What are all the ways you can re-use or re-purpose your intellectual property? Re-purposing your intellectual property so that you can offer it as educational material for prospects or products for sales are some examples. Here's another: Richard Branson has leveraged the Virgin brand to the point where he literally has hundreds of businesses using the Virgin name and every one of them generates cash for him, whenever a Virgin branded product is sold."

"That's a lot of great leveraging examples – inspiring too."

"There's more: How about trade secrets? If you own some unique know-how, can you license it to people who don't compete with you? What about your client base? Are you only selling customers one thing, or only selling them what you can make? What else can you sell them that's complementary to what you do? Are there people who would like to sell products to your customer base? Referrals are also a way of leveraging your client base and the good will of your customers. If you have unconverted leads that you know you will not buy what you sell, why not sell them to someone else who might be able to close them? Or you might consider a joint venture and do it on a profit sharing basis."

"What about our marketing program?"

"Your marketing is highly leverage-able. It often costs nothing to take a modestly performing marketing activity and turn it into a winner. Most of us accept whatever result we get, but the key to success is to constantly ratchet up performance with continuous testing of small incremental improvements."

He took a sip of coffee, then continued: What about other people's assets, how can you leverage those? Much like the fellow I described, you can leverage another's investment in their customer base. How many thousands or hundreds of thousands of dollars have they spent in building their client base? If you can do a joint venture with people who are successful in your target market, you can tap into that investment immediately without anything like the expense it would take to build it on your own. What's more you are tapping into a customer base that is predisposed to buying, as they are already buying from your joint venture partner."

Another sip of coffee and he resumed. "Many businesses have intellectual property they don't sell, but would be happy to give it away in order to promote themselves. How can you access this information to provide something of value to your own customers? As you see the list is endless. Use leverage as the key to growing your business. Align yourself with non-competing businesses whose goods and services complement your own to obtain introductions to their clients, who can then become your clients. Or, find other ways to access the customer base of firm's whose clients might have use of your services. This can save a tremendous amount of time and money when compared with the costs of establishing such a customer base from scratch."

"What's the best way to get started?"

"Begin to look around for opportunities to multiply the effect of what you do. Don't settle for anything just because most of the people in your industry do it that way. Find a new way to do it that provides you with leverage."

"Thank you, as always, for your terrific advice and insightful suggestions," Lindsay beamed. "I'm really sorry this is our last scheduled meeting – you've been an outstanding mentor to me."

"Then, let's expand our discussion of leverage to include mentors, as using a mentor is a highly effective use of leverage – you're in essence using the expertise of another to help catapult you forward far further than you'd ever likely get on your own accord. It sounds like you'd like to carry on with the help of a mentor and I won't be in town for the most part as I'll be traveling for up to a month at a time – and I have commitments to keep when I do get back in town…"

"So, I need to consider finding another mentor," Lindsay pondered, sadly. "Can you help me out with this search?"

"Of course I can, Lindsay. Let me frame this by stating that the leverage you obtain from mentors can provide a shortcut to great success in your business. Let me relate a personal experience. I woke up one morning with a revelation about my business. It was so simple; I couldn't believe it had taken me two years to figure it out. The interesting thing was that despite huge amounts of time thinking about this challenge, the actual answer came to me in a split second. I was reflecting on a discussion with a successful business person while at the gym the day before. He didn't give me the answer but his insight pointed me in the right direction."

Lindsay leaned forward. "Go on," she invited.

"Well, I had made the mistake of not discussing my challenge with anyone else until that time in the gym. I felt the problem was something I should have known the answer to, so I didn't really feel comfortable talking about it to others. Wow, did I learn the value of having a mentor – this fellow's insight really helped. I have probably lost 18 months of productivity simply because I wouldn't ask for help. How often have you said to yourself, 'I wish I knew then what I know now?' That's how I felt after keeping the problem to myself for over a year before turning to a mentor and being put on the right track to having it quickly resolved."

"Of course," Lindsay smiled broadly, "I've learned from our time together that mentors – present company included – can make an enormous difference."

"They sure can, Lindsay. It takes a long time to become successful. Along the way there are many pitfalls. Each time we encounter a pitfall, we learn something, regardless of the outcome. This means that if you make a point of getting advice from someone experienced in your area of interest, you can probably avoid most of the common mistakes and often you can find short cuts to success by following the advice you get from the voices of experience. No matter who you are and where you are in your career, finding yourself good mentors can be invaluable. I like to have different mentors for different aspects of my life – both business and personal – and there are a number of people I look to as mentors. There's lots of research proving the great value of mentoring relationships, and I firmly believe that a lot of my success today is due to some important mentors in my past.

"Can you give an example?" Lindsay asked.

"In my first real job, I was a medical technologist working in the local medical school. Here I learned the value of delegating tasks and letting people run with them and not interfering. Although I was only 18, my boss – who served as something of a mentor to me – kept testing me by giving me bigger challenges, letting me make my mistakes and helping me learn from them. From my very first managerial position, I have always tried to manage people this way. Managing people like this helps the eagles fly, while the mediocre players flounder."

The StreetSmart Marketer paused for a sip of coffee, then continued. "In another position, I learned that simple tasks are not simple unless you understand the secrets. I was struggling as a novice salesman. My boss was an expert salesman and sold almost effortlessly by asking a series of questions. To the uninitiated, this simply looked like having a nice chat and being inquisitive."

"But it was more than that?"

"Yes. It was only once he started explaining the strategy to me that I discovered he had an overall game plan. He used a sophisticated technique comprised of four different types of questions that yielded very different results depending on how and when they were used in the conversation. He also showed me how to use questions to build trust, to understand needs, to handle objections and even to close the sale. To this day I still sell this way. I have literally made hundreds of thousands of dollars with this one technique. I got it free, but in retrospect I would have paid many thousands of dollars to learn it. In fact had I not learned to sell this way, I think I might have had a very different career. I have never again assumed that what looks simple is simple."

"I'm beginning to think that not having a mentor makes no sense as you're only denying yourself growth and opportunity," Lindsay observed.

"That's a very astute observation. Many of us become satisfied with a certain level of performance, assuming that it is enough. We become complacent with our level of performance and stop looking for answers. This often cheats us; we miss the opportunities for growth, not realizing that some simple changes can turn a project from a failure or marginal success to a runaway success with no extra cost and often no extra effort."

"That added success is with the help of a mentor."

"That's exactly right, Lindsay. You may not know what you need to learn to make the next leap in performance and skill. But the great thing is; there is no subject you need to learn that you can't find out about from someone else who has been there and done it successfully before. One of your goals should be to find people who can help you move forward. It will accelerate your results and make a big difference in your performance."

"But how do you find mentors?"

"First off, you should write down the goals you want to achieve. Then decide where you need help. Once you have that list, look around in your industry for people who are successful. Ideally try to find people who have retired recently. They are often at loose ends; bored with doing nothing and willing to help. Also, if their retirement is recent, they are still current, which is critical. Another source is subject matter experts in the field you need to learn about."

"Once I've found a mentor or a potential mentor, how do I... raise the idea of possible mentorship," Lindsay queried.

"The easiest way to reach these people is to write them a short letter, expressing admiration for their careers and achievements. This must be quite sincere as any insincerity will be immediately recognizable. Ask for the opportunity to meet with them, perhaps over lunch and outline the area or issue on which you are looking for advice. This first meeting should be exploratory. You need to know if you get along, and understand what this person can teach you. You also need to find out your potential mentor's level of interest in this kind of role. You also need to understand what he or she wants in return and what each of you expects from the relationship. I would not discuss compensation until you are sure you want to work together."

Lindsay nodded agreement. "I'll have to come up with some good questions to determine if we make a good fit."

"Well, some questions you should have in the back of your mind include: Is this someone you can trust? Is this someone you can confide in? Is this someone who can give you relevant advice, feedback and support? Is this someone with sufficient technical knowledge to be able to help you learn what you need to learn?"

"What about the costs involved?"

"Be prepared to pay top dollar for this kind of help. After all, these people can help you accelerate your progress dramatically and you can learn from every mistake they have made. Imagine what it would have been worth to me to have solved my problem in a matter of days or weeks instead of years! But don't pay more than you are comfortable with. Follow your instincts."

"I'm just wondering how to best approach the meetings."

"Before each meeting decide what you want from the discussion and outline this before you begin. This also will give you a measure of success. When working with your mentor, it is important to keep track of your progress so that both of you can see the benefits of working together. It will also be important to let your mentor know what you are learning as you progress through the relationship."

"There are a lot of talented people out there – it's going to be difficult choosing which one to go with as a mentor," Lindsay considered.

"Why limit yourself to just one mentor? I believe in multiple mentors. I like to choose people with different skill-sets and perspectives. This not only gives me depth in the chosen area, but also the opportunity to compare different perspectives where appropriate. Sometimes the people you would like to have as mentors are already in the business of giving advice. If this is the case, respect that. This is how they earn their living; don't expect them to do something for you outside of what they normally do. If you need their skills and can afford to pay for them, often this is a great way to accelerate your success."

"And it's a way I'll definitely be taking," Lindsay confirmed. "I'd also like to keep you as one of my mentors, even if it's just on an occasional basis whenever you have time to spare. And I'd be very interested in having you hold seminars and motivational information events for our staff. I can't begin to tell you the difference your advice has made to our printing business. Thank you so much..."

"And thank you, Lindsay – you've been a good sounding board for some of the thoughts I was stringing together for seminars and business meetings. Your questions helped me frame concepts in a more concise manner. And it's been a real pleasure watching your confidence grow and your business succeed. Unfortunately, I have a plane to catch and I really should go."

With that, the two friends parted paths with plans to catch up with each other at a future date – at their favourite park bench.

KEY 11:
Leverage and Mentoring

1. Use leverage as the key to growing your business. Align yourself with non-competing businesses whose goods and services complement your own to obtain introductions to their clients, who can then become your clients. Or, find other ways to access the customer base of firm's whose clients might have use of your services. This can save a tremendous amount of time and money when compared with the costs of establishing such a customer base from scratch.

2. Leverage is widely misunderstood, but it can be the key that unlocks the door to growing your business. Leverage is simply the ability to create a large return with a small amount of effort. You can get leverage on your own assets and you can get leverage on other peoples' assets.

3. Every asset we have is leverage-able. Time is being the scarcest and most important asset for entrepreneurs to master. But what else can we leverage? How about under-utilized assets like intellectual property. Re-purposing your intellectual property so that you can offer it as educational material for prospects or as products for sales are some examples.

4. Begin to look around for opportunities to multiply the effect of what you do. Don't settle for anything just because most of the people in your industry do it that way. Find a new way to do it that provides you with leverage.

5. Getting advice from someone experienced in your area of interest can help you avoid most of the common mistakes and often you can find short cuts to success. No matter whom you are and where you are in your career, finding good mentors can be invaluable.

6. Using a mentor is a highly effective use of leverage – you're in essence using the expertise of another to help catapult you forward far further than you'd ever likely get on your own accord.

7. There is no subject you need to learn that you can't find out about from someone else who has been there and done it successfully before. One of your goals should be to find people who can help you move forward. It will accelerate your results and make a big difference in your performance.

Epilogue:
Lindsay's Lessons:

Lindsay watched the StreetSmart Marketer walk briskly through the park to catch his flight. Then, she turned and began heading back to her office, racing across the street to avoid traffic.

As she approached the office building, she thought of everything that had been accomplished over the summer: Sales reps were focusing foremost on customers, expanding buying behaviour and amassing client lists and referrals.

Sales revenue and profit were both up. The *You Marketing* strategies were getting big results and compliments were abundant on the effectiveness of advertising campaigns and customer relations. She knew in her heart she'd done a remarkable job in turning the print shop around, getting it in good shape for her father's expected return in a week's time. She also knew her dad was set in his ways and might not appreciate the changes, regardless of how effective they were.

As she entered the building, she caught a glimpse of her father's portrait in the hall and tears welled in her eyes. He *must* get well enough to return, she thought. His life was his company. At least the print shop was running smoothly. It had survived – and thrived – in a remarkably short turnaround time.

Walking down the hall, she heard voices chattering and a familiar raspy, booming voice filling the meeting room. She stepped in the room and found Jack Roberts regaling the crowd with stories of his adventures in the hospital.

The room fell silent as he stopped talking and peered at the end of the room. "Lindsay," he said, "I want to talk to you."

Lindsay approached her dad, her heart pounding in nervous anticipation.

"I think it's in this company's best interests," he began, "that you be removed from the acting president position," "And," he quickly added, "that you are appointed fulltime president."

"Are you sure?"

"Of course, I'm sure," he said, giving her a hug. "You've earned it. I can't believe how much more successful our little print shop is now. You've got a sales boom happening – we're going to have to hire more people to keep up. I couldn't have achieved this much in a million years. Thank you so very much."

"What are *you* going to do?"

"Me? I've appointed myself president emeritus in charge of deep thoughts on the golf course. I may call in from time to time to share my wisdom – or I may not. One thing I do know: I'm leaving this company in very capable hands."

The gathering erupted in sustained applause as Jack handed his daughter the keys to his legendary desk drawer liquor cabinet. "For when you're entertaining guests," he whispered in her ear. "You've already got keys to the front door and my – your – office. Enjoy the promotion – and take some time off to relax, will you?"

"I will," Lindsay promised him. "I'm working that into my strategic time allocation."

"Your what?"

"My... vacation time."

"Good, you do that... whatever... location. When my ticker took a tumble I learned the hard way that life's too short to spend all your time at the office. You need to get out and enjoy yourself. You know, there's a park not far from here..."

Complete Summary
11 Low-Cost Keys that Unlock the Secrets
To Rapid Growth in Your Business

KEY 1: Ideal Prospects: Summary

1. In all markets there are ideal buyers that are easier to sell than all other buyers. Focus your resources mainly on ideal buyers, as they're more profitable, easier to serve and more ready to buy.

2. Ensure prospects buy from you and not your competition, by tailoring your approach to fit their needs. Instead of pestering them with calls asking them if they're ready to buy, keep in touch with them by providing useful information they can use. You then emerge as their first choice when they are ready to do business.

3. Understand that marketing is everything a business does to acquire and keep customers; then work to make your marketing efforts more effective.

4. Networking and referrals are part of marketing. These two tactics are often the default for people who have no marketing strategy or process. While these tactics can create quite a successful business, they eventually limit your growth because ultimately the amount of networking you can do is limited. When you're networking you can't deliver, and when you're delivering, you don't have time to network. If these are your only marketing tools, it will be extremely difficult to grow business beyond a few people.

5. Networking and referrals have lots of hidden costs that are actually marketing costs. For example, lunches, dinners, coffee, membership fees, meeting attendance, your time, travel etc. Don't be fooled into thinking your time is free. It isn't. And remember, there is also an opportunity cost to doing these things.

6. By doing all these activities, costs mount up and you will be surprised to discover how much a new customer really costs you, even with these seemingly free activities.

7. Whether you acknowledge it or not, your business buys customers. The first step is to recognise that you have invested considerable sums of money over the years of building your business and understand that marketing is simply a way of buying customers. For some people this may sound distasteful, but you should try to get used to it.

8. Marketing and client acquisition is an investment. In order to protect that investment, you have to do everything to ensure that once acquired, a customer comes back regularly to buy more. This is true in businesses where clients only buy once or occasionally. Even in businesses where marketing is restricted to networking and referrals, client acquisition is still the most expensive thing you do. The best way to protect this investment is to fall in love with your customer rather than with your product or service. Falling in love with your customer will ensure you provide service that is without peer.

KEY 2: The Unwritten Marketing Rule

1. Realize that simply offering a valuable service or product is not enough to succeed. You need to market your product or service to bring customers to you.

2. Figure out what makes your business different or unique. Then, differentiate yourself from competitors. Advertising and marketing that's the same as everyone else's does as much for your competitors as it does for you. Marketing making the same claims as everyone else, forces customers to focus on one thing they do understand; price. This leads to an eroding of margins and a lack of customer loyalty.

3. To generate leads, use a combination of strategies, such as starting a referral program, utilizing direct mail campaigns and developing alliances with businesses whose services complement your own.

4. If you cannot find the time to personally deal with incoming business sales and opportunities, hire an assistant to take on some of the load. It's a false economy to think you're saving money by not hiring – when in fact an assistant may well secure sales revenue far in excess of their salary.

5. Strive to increase sales by improving your product or service. You can effectively do this by first asking yourself a series of questions concerning ways the product might be improved, from lowering the price to adding features and benefits that add value and desirability.

6. Avoid having your marketing efforts lost in the clutter of unwanted advertising messages and sales pitches. Instead, get to know your prospects and customers; provide them with gifts of value – such as information they can use, educate them on the value of your service – *then* sell them.

7. Tailor the free information reports you send customers to meet their needs and concerns. But don't send such reports unsolicited. Get the client to request the report. This gives you an excuse to follow up in a friendly manner with more information that helps educate the customer into becoming a better buyer while matching them with the right products and services, virtually guaranteeing repeat business.

8. Practice *You Marketing* focusing on the customer's needs and goals rather than *Me Marketing* focusing on how highly you think of your products and services. The customers and prospects don't care if you think you're the best; what they do care about is whether what you're offering meets their specific needs and will help them achieve success. Don't be guilty of bragging to the bored.

9. Success is built on positive relationships: People buy from people they like, and we generally like people who are interested in us and our needs. In most cases, as potential buyers, we're completely selfish and will only engage if we find something or someone to be interesting. Successful salespeople quickly learn that you can't be interesting unless you are interested.

10. The best way to demonstrate interest is to ask insightful questions as they ultimately provide insightful answers in marketing communications that show customers why you are the logical choice to solve burning problems. Once StreetSmart Marketers understand these challenges they use their knowledge and skills to raise perception about potential solutions. Only then do they introduce the product or service and what it can do for the client.

KEY 3:
Fix the Product or Service First

1. You can't expect marketing to save a "me too" product or service. You have to be the buyers' first choice. Firms with generic or deficient products or services must find ways to understand what their market niche wants; then find ways to make the offer more compelling to prospects.

2. Falling in love with your product can be dangerous to your wealth: Don't be blind to risks. If your product is untried, make sure it can find a market. Do market research.

3. Even if your idea is a good one, you're not going get far unless other people like it too and are willing to purchase or invest in making it happen. People vote with their cash.

4. Figure out what makes your business different or unique. Then, differentiate yourself from competitors. Advertising and marketing that's the same as everyone else's does as much for your competitors as it does for you. Marketing making the same claims as everyone else, forces customers to focus on one thing they do understand; price. This leads to an eroding of margins and a lack of customer loyalty.

5. Use key word search software tools such as Overture and Wordtracker to surf the Internet and find buyer trends.

6. Buy a competitor's products or services and then correct their flaws in your own product or service.

7. Become your own customer by opening your packaging and testing your products and services much like one of your customers. Then, improve/correct any flaws found.

KEY 4:
Sell the Bait first

1. Interesting and effective newsletters are hard work and are written from the readers' point of view.

2. When a customer says "no" to your sales pitch, ask her why. Then listen carefully and respectfully to her answer. Take notes. This information is likely to contain the clues you need to improve your offer. Get back in touch once your offer has been improved.

3. Make sure your customer's details are in your database, and begin to nurture the relationship. If you know what her interests are, or what challenges she is facing, you can send relevant articles from time to time. Send her your newsletter and other information of value to build trust.

4. To catch ideal buyers you have to use the right bait. People are resistant to being sold, but if you can first offer something free that your prospects want, you have a better chance of engaging them and selling them something.

5. Find ways of delivering value to get people's attention, such as inviting prospects to an event where they'll learn something that will make them more successful.

6. Wow your customers with polite, friendly professional service that will make them want to choose you over competitors.

7. Ask for referrals but also earn by doing a great job that the client appreciates so he'll recommend your services.

8. Understand the difference between networking and sales and then practice effective networking to build future sales.

KEY 5:
Wooing Prospects

1. Marketing, like dating, shouldn't be rushed. Marketers who ask for too big a commitment early on risk frightening otherwise interested parties. Advertisers who try to make a sale without a full description of the offer risk losing customers that don't see the value of what's being offered.

2. The key with marketing is to understand that no matter how much success you have with a program, you owe it to yourself to continually find ways to improve your results. You can often get dramatic increases with only very minor changes that cost nothing."

3. Making the easy sale first usually involves offering something free. Let the customer try out your services at no risk. So, what can you offer for free without breaking the bank? The simplest gift is information. The best kind of information is the kind that helps the customer avoid making bad buying decisions, or protects them from dangers they might not even be aware of.

4. It's not enough that you have a great product or service; you need to show customers how you can help them solve a problem.

5. Stop talking about yourself and listen to the customer. Don't fall in love with your product – fall in love with your customer instead. Meeting their needs means sales.

6. Testimonials are critical for new products and services. Social proof is very effective in encouraging undecided people to move forward.

7. Use extended payment terms, guarantees, time-limited offers and other incentives. Make it easy for clients to buy.

KEY 6:
Risk Reversal

1. Realize that Risk causes hesitation, and hesitation kills sales, so shoulder the risk. Guarantees are one of the most effective ways of doing this, but you have to put them out front so people know you stand by what you are selling.

2. One way to reverse the risk is to offer an unconditional money back guarantee, if certain results are not achieved.

3. If you already offer an informal guarantee, why not build it into your marketing program to build trust and sales?

4. Most people will not abuse a guarantee and it's a very effective way of securing customer loyalty.

5. Offer customers a gift for trying your product or service. If they are dissatisfied, they will receive a full refund, but they also get to keep the gift.

6. A guarantee encourages unhappy customers to contact you. Instead of bad-mouthing your product, unhappy customers call and explain their problem – giving you an opportunity to fix things.

7. Changing your focus from selling to serving customers can make difference in building your client base later on.

KEY 7:
Creating effective advertising:

1. Marketing for small business isn't a beauty contest. You should really run only direct response, not image advertising. Direct response is 100 per cent measurable and if done properly, you get the image advertising free.

2. Simply changing a headline has been shown to double or triple response rates and in some cases improve response rates by up to 21 times.

3. Effective advertising is like a soap opera: each sentence should leave you wanting more, so you read the next sentence to see what happens.

4. You not only need a great headline; you need to know the underlying needs, fears, desires and wants of your target market, and include the information in your copy.

5. If you don't create instant interest and value, people won't read even the shortest letter. Creating interest and value can get the longest letters read more than once.

6. Social proof is one of the most powerful tools available to the direct response marketer. Use lots of testimonials showing that you can deliver what you claim. People want to know that you can deliver what you claim. Other proof mechanisms include specific details, numbers. The more specific you are, the more your claims will be believed.

7. Write to people in a personal manner. Write to them in the same way you speak to people. Worry more about clearly communicating your message than the quality of your English prose. Use slang, use contractions and remember in copywriting it's OK to begin a sentence with "And."

8. Continually find ways of producing better results from the same or fewer resources. As a business owner you owe it to yourself to ensure that every marketing activity yields the maximum output.

9. Everyone is secretly asking to be lead, so tell your prospects exactly what action to take to buy from you and show them how easy it is to order.

KEY 8:
Expanding Buying Behaviour

1. Once a customer has bought from you, expand buying behavior as they're predisposed to buy again. Expanding buying behavior means up-selling or cross-selling at the point of sale, it means programming sales in advance and it means offering other products and services as a back end stream of revenue to maximize the customer relationship.

2. The quickest way to grow your business is not by adding new customers, but by encouraging existing customers to buy more or buy more often.

3. To increase profits, trim low-profit-margin items from your product line. They may be eating up limited and valuable resources that could be better utilized elsewhere.

4. Business owners must always look for ways to increase the dollar amount at the point of purchase, or offer existing customers a reason to come back more often.

5. Getting each and every one of your customers to spend just 10 per cent more each time they buy from you, can have a tremendous impact on your bottom line.

KEY 9:

Repeat Mailings and Free Reports:

1. If you only send a mailing out once you are only getting a fraction of what's possible in terms of response..

2. Figure out what makes your business different or unique. Then, differentiate yourself from competitors. Advertising and marketing that's the same as everyone else's does as much for your competitors as it does for you. Marketing making the same claims as everyone else, forces customers to focus on one thing they do understand; price. This leads to an eroding of margins and a lack of customer loyalty.

3. Mailings that arrive fast and furiously don't negatively affect customer relationships and in fact increase your business.

4. The real problem with many of the people who have tried a particular strategy and found it produced no results, is that they wrongly assumed they knew what to do.

5. If you try to sell everything, you sell nothing. If you try to sell everyone you sell nobody.

6. Never try to sell something in a medium where you can't afford to tell the whole story. Prospects need information to make buying decisions, and unless you give it to them they won't buy.

7. Without paying anything more, yo0u can get great results from a revamped ad with a compelling headline to draw people in and clear instruction on placing orders.

8. Before you execute your next marketing activity, invest the time to learn how to do it right – or hire an expert. That way you will generate a much better result.

KEY 10:
Strategic Time Allocation

1. Force yourself to reduce your workload by guarding your time. This is all about setting some reasonable expectations for yourself. For example, instead of working every weekend, guard your weekends jealously.

2. If you focus on too many things, you achieve little. If you chase two rabbits they both get away. You have to decide what really matters to you.

3. You don't just *find* time for important things – you have to *make* time.

4. As a business owner, you have to decide what's most important, and work on that. You can't afford to get sidetracked by what's easy, or fun or less stressful. You have to decide what is most important and do it, or get it done.

5. Most small businesses are strapped for resources, be it money, people or equipment. But this should not stop you. You can get almost anything you want if you are resourceful. Somebody always has what you need, so once you find them there are many ways to get what you need. Try barter and joint ventures for starters.

6. Part of problem-solving involves searching for better questions – because these can lead to better answers. Ask yourself why when examining a problem and with each answer ask who again, five times in total.

7. If you would like to read more than you do, but don't have the time, consider reading book summaries. Most books only contain one or two principle ideas. These and the key points can usually be captured and distilled into a short summary.

8. Manage Your Time Strategically. As a business owner you have choices over how you spend your time. For example, there is 'preparation time' that is for delegating tasks, planning your strategies and tactics.

9. Everything you do in business makes a difference and has an impact; good or bad.

10. Each day, take a look at each of your scheduled tasks and decide if your business will suffer if you don't do it. If the answer is no, just don't do it.

11. Effective problem-solvers take action early and decisively, mostly with little concern over making the wrong decision. This is in sharp contrast to some people who find that until they can see the whole situation, they tend to do nothing and this can mean a long time of inaction on something that needs immediate attention.

KEY 11:
Leverage and Mentoring

1. Use leverage as the key to growing your business. Align yourself with non-competing businesses whose goods and services complement your own to obtain introductions to their clients, who can then become your clients. Or, find other ways to access the customer base of firm's whose clients might have use of your services. This can save a tremendous amount of time and money when compared with the costs of establishing such a customer base from scratch.

2. Leverage is widely misunderstood, but it can be the key that unlocks the door to growing your business. Leverage is simply the ability to create a large return with a small amount of effort. You can get leverage on your own assets and you can get leverage on other peoples' assets.

3. Every asset we have is leverage-able. Time is being the scarcest and most important asset for entrepreneurs to master. But what else can we leverage? How about under-utilized assets like intellectual property. Re-purposing your intellectual property so that you can offer it as educational material for prospects or as products for sales are some examples.

4. Begin to look around for opportunities to multiply the effect of what you do. Don't settle for anything just because most of the people in your industry do it that way. Find a new way to do it that provides you with leverage.

5. Getting advice from someone experienced in your area of interest can help you avoid most of the common mistakes and often you can find short cuts to success. No matter whom you are and where you are in your career, finding good mentors can be invaluable.

6. Using a mentor is a highly effective use of leverage – you're in essence using the expertise of another to help catapult you forward far further than you'd ever likely get on your own accord.

7. There is no subject you need to learn that you can't find out about from someone else who has been there and done it successfully before. One of your goals should be to find people who can help you move forward. It will accelerate your results and make a big difference in your performance.

And for more information...

StreetSmart Marketing
High-return low-risk growth strategies guaranteed to make any owner-operated business grow.

Training, Mentoring and Consulting
Michael Hepworth is available for telephone and in-person consultations on your marketing and business growth questions. Reach him at info@streetsmartmarketer.com.

Sign up for his free bi-weekly newsletter loaded with practical business building advice at streetsmartmarketer.com

Speeches
Michael gives rousing educational speeches, using stories and perspectives gathered during more than 30 years of practical business building. Because of his practical "been there, done that" approach, business owners give his talks rave reviews

Call today 1-866-565-1941

Manor House Publishing Inc.
www.manor-house.biz 905-648-2193

www.ingramcontent.com/pod-product-compliance
Lightning Source LLC
Chambersburg PA
CBHW021104210326
41598CB00016B/1329